Sonnets of Catharina von Greiffenberg

UNC | COLLEGE OF ARTS AND SCIENCES
Germanic and Slavic Languages and Literatures

From 1949 to 2004, UNC Press and the UNC Department of Germanic & Slavic Languages and Literatures published the UNC Studies in the Germanic Languages and Literatures series. Monographs, anthologies, and critical editions in the series covered an array of topics including medieval and modern literature, theater, linguistics, philology, onomastics, and the history of ideas. Through the generous support of the National Endowment for the Humanities and the Andrew W. Mellon Foundation, books in the series have been reissued in new paperback and open access digital editions. For a complete list of books visit www.uncpress.org.

Sonnets of Catharina von Greiffenberg
Methods of Composition

FLORA KIMMICH

UNC Studies in the Germanic Languages and Literatures
Number 83

Copyright © 1975

This work is licensed under a Creative Commons CC BY-NC-ND license. To view a copy of the license, visit http://creativecommons.org/licenses.

Suggested citation: Kimmich, Flora. *Sonnets of Catharina von Greiffenberg: Methods of Composition*. Chapel Hill: University of North Carolina Press, 1975. DOI: https://doi.org/10.5149/9781469657639_Kimmich

Library of Congress Cataloging-in-Publication Data
Names: Kimmich, Flora.
Title: Sonnets of Catharina von Greiffenberg : Methods of composition / by Flora Kimmich.
Other titles: University of North Carolina Studies in the Germanic Languages and Literatures ; no. 83.
Description: Chapel Hill : University of North Carolina Press, [1975] Series: University of North Carolina Studies in the Germanic Languages and Literatures. | Includes bibliographical references and index.
Identifiers: LCCN 74031031 | ISBN 978-1-4696-5762-2 (pbk: alk. paper) | ISBN 978-1-4696-5763-9 (ebook)
Subjects: Greiffenberg, Catharina Regina von, 1633-1694. | Geistliche Sonnette. | Gryphius, Andreas, 1616-1664. | Sonnets.
Classification: LCC PT1729 .G83 G435 | DCC 831/ .5

ACKNOWLEDGMENTS

It is a pleasure to record my debts. A fellowship of the American Association of University Women, 1965-1966, permitted me to begin to study Greiffenberg and to visit the Archive of the Germanisches Nationalmuseum, Nürnberg. The staff of the Archive assisted me generously and with great courtesy. Excerpts from letters of Hans Rudolf von Greiffenberg and Johann Wilhelm von Stubenberg appear here with the kind permission of the Museum. The Stadtbibliothek, Nürnberg, furnished me with copies of its material on Greiffenberg. The editors of *Euphorion* permitted me to republish in Chapter Seven a revised version of material which appeared under the title "Nochmals zur Umarbeitung der Sonette von Andreas Gryphius" in *Euphorion*, 68 (1974), 296-317.

Curt von Faber du Faur allowed me to use the Yale copy of the *Geistliche Sonnette*. Hedwig Dejon, to whose care the Faber Collection was entrusted after his death, gave me access to the final edition of Gryphius' sonnets. Blake Lee Spahr lent me a copy of Horst Frank's unpublished dissertation. Victor Lange encouraged and advised me in placing the manuscript with a publisher. Theodore Ziolkowski sponsored my petition to the Princeton University Committee on Research in the Humanities and Social Sciences, which helped me generously with the cost of publication.

Heinrich Henel watched over the essay from the beginning. He read the manuscript with great care, giving me full benefit of his insight into the sonnets and of his knowledge of the literary tradition. His friendship and his interest in my work have accompanied me for many years.

My husband Christoph shared my task from the murky days of our first acquaintance with Greiffenberg. I imposed upon his patience, appealed to his judgment, and required his clear intelligence. The book is a record of his unfailing response.

CONTENTS

I	Of Problems and Method	1
II	Greiffenberg and the Sonnets	9
III	The Linear Poems	24
IV	Repetition	40
V	Amassment and Assimilation	56
VI	The Integrated Sonnets	72
VII	Greiffenberg and Gryphius	97
VIII	Instead of a Conclusion	120
	Bibliography	123
	Index of Sonnets: Greiffenberg and Gryphius	126

CHAPTER ONE

OF PROBLEMS AND METHOD

My undertaking here is rather a humble one—to explore a collection of sonnets by a poet whose name is familiar but whose work is virtually unexamined. The essay keeps to this task. It refrains from drawing conclusions on the mentality of the poet; it makes no generalizations about the literary epoch in which these sonnets appeared; it attempts no history of the sonnet. Of all these enterprises I am a bit skeptical for the moment. For I doubt that we have enough accurate information for such enlargement, reluctant as we have been to look long and thoughtfully at the texts of German Baroque poetry. We have inclined instead to use the texts as supporting evidence for other arguments.

Modern scholarship on the German Baroque began with an essay on the style of the lyric poetry, published by Fritz Strich in 1916.[1] Strich's purpose is to establish the seventeenth century as a distinct literary epoch. He demonstrates his observations about the style of the period upon selected features of lyric texts—antithesis, pointe, word play. He expands upon his findings to relate Baroque poetry to the poetry of Sturm und Drang and the Romantic period (and to the Germanic spirit at large), using as his bridge the relationship between the poem and the poet's experience. Here begins a scholarly tradition. As Richard Alewyn has pointed out, a great service of these early studies of Baroque style is that they taught us to examine linguistic phenomena apart from their contents and in connection with the significance of their structure and function.[2] The early studies also began a practice of treating these phenomena apart from the specific settings in which they occur. And Strich's bold statements about Baroque poems and the experience of the poet introduced a custom of considering Baroque lyric poetry in the light of the poetry which appeared late in the following century—of what is called *Erlebnisdichtung*.

Gerhard Fricke's study of Andreas Gryphius, published 1933, is directed toward demonstrating and defining the difference between the earlier and the later poetry, in defense of Baroque poetry against anachronistic reproaches for coldness and incongruence.[3] Fricke con-

---

[1] Fritz Strich, "Der lyrische Stil des 17. Jahrhunderts," *Abhandlungen zur deutschen Literaturgeschichte. Franz Muncker zum 60. Geburtstag dargebracht* (München, 1916), reprinted in *Deutsche Barockforschung*, ed. Richard Alewyn (Köln, 1965), pp. 229-59.
[2] Alewyn, *Deutsche Barockforschung*, p. 10.
[3] Gerhard Fricke, *Die Bildlichkeit in der Dichtung des Andreas Gryphius* (Berlin, 1933).

siders a selected feature of the text—imagery—within a system of opposed principles: subjectivity versus objectivity, the personal versus the representative, symbol versus allegory. His method has the virtues and the vices of contrastive analysis. It illuminates dramatically how Baroque poetry differs from the poetry of the succeeding period and permits precise description of the difference. But it uses a system of antinomies derived from a theory of poetry more appropriate to the later period, and it is not equipped to observe how Baroque poetry fares outside this set of contrasts.

Hans Pyritz's examination of Paul Fleming's love poetry, published in 1932, assumes a different bearing on the problem of Baroque poetry and *Erlebnisdichtung*.[4] Pyritz posits the distinction and works anterior to it, exploring Petrarchism, one of the literary traditions which converged in this poetry, and its emergence in the motifs of Fleming's work. In his closing chapters Pyritz juxtaposes Fleming's poetry and the theory of *Erlebnisdichtung* at length. Here again we find the limitations of a theory not appropriate to the earlier poetry: Pyritz searches for a relationship between a poem and an experience of the poet and overlooks the possibility of a poem which functions apart from this relationship.

Recent work on the German Baroque lyric lies in the succession of Pyritz and Fricke. Both Karl Otto Conrady and Dietrich Walther Jöns examine traditions which contributed to the poetry—Conrady the Latin tradition since the classical period and Jöns the emblematic tradition—and each concerns himself with selected features of poetic texts—Conrady with rhetorical figures and Jöns with emblematic motifs.[5] Both elaborate on the difference between lyric poetry of the Baroque and of a later period. Neither undertakes to examine a text comprehensively. To these studies and to the scholarly tradition to which they belong we owe a wealth of finely perceived information on the prevalent assumptions in the seventeenth century and the special processes at work in the literature. Without this knowledge we cannot understand the Baroque. Among other things, it protects against incommensurate, uninformed, or airily speculative attempts to construe the literature. To say that there are certain questions that these studies do not raise and certain competences of literature which they do not see is not a categorical reproach but merely the old observation that every system of inquiry has its own horizons and none is exhaustive.

In 1949 Erich Trunz published a study of five sonnets by Andreas

---

[4] Hans Pyritz, *Paul Flemings Liebeslyrik: Zur Geschichte des Petrarkismus* (Göttingen, 1965).
[5] Karl Otto Conrady, *Lateinische Dichtungstradition und deutsche Lyrik des 17. Jahrhunderts* (Bonn, 1962); Dietrich Walther Jöns, *Das "Sinnen-Bild": Studien zur allegorischen Bildlichkeit bei Andreas Gryphius* (Stuttgart, 1966).

Gryphius which lies outside the mainstream of German scholarship.[6] Trunz examines the texts of the sonnets comprehensively and offers what might be described best as readings of the poems. His effort has had no successors. Probably by no accident, a subsequent study of Gryphius' sonnets as whole texts was written by an American, Marvin Schindler.[7] Like Trunz, Schindler examines several sonnets independently. Unlike Trunz, he inquires not only into a poem's meaning and style, but also specifically into the poet's craft. He describes his procedure as a combination of explanation and interpretation. Schindler questions Gryphius' sonnets from a perspective not used on them before, he asks questions not addressed to them before, and he receives answers we have not heard before. Doubtless his claims for the primacy of the text are overstated. Nonetheless, an approach such as his holds possibilities of great fruitfulness. As evidence I would cite Stephen Booth's immensely sophisticated exploration of Shakespeare's craft at sonnets, descendant of an English and American scholarly tradition which has bent its efforts on interpretation of texts, even while it has not neglected ideas, conventions, and modes of thought in literature.[8]

Scholarship in Catharina von Greiffenberg is neither extensive nor very distinguished. It has suffered either from slackness or from misplaced rigor. To the first group belong the work of Hermann Uhde-Bernays, who broached the archival materials on Greiffenberg in 1903, and Leo Villiger.[9] Both have cast their efforts broadly. They touch upon the poet's life, her thought, and her poems and examine none of these carefully. To this first group belongs also the most recent piece on Greiffenberg, Malve Kristin Slocum's dissertation, which treats the motifs *Lob* and *Spiel* in the sonnets in a fashion akin to paraphrase.[10] Misdirected rigor appears in the second part of a dissertation by Horst Frank and in the dissertation of Peter Maurice Daly.[11] Frank classifies Greiffenberg's sonnets according to their direction of address—whether toward a human ear, toward God, or toward no explicit listener—and according to their intention—whether to praise, to teach, or to speak of

---

[6] Erich Trunz, "Fünf Sonette des Andreas Gryphius: Versuch einer Auslegung," *Vom Geist der Dichtung: Gedächtnisschrift für Robert Petsch,* ed. Fritz Martini (Hamburg, 1949), pp. 180-205.

[7] Marvin S. Schindler, *Sonnets of Andreas Gryphius: Use of the Poetic Word in the Seventeenth Century* (Gainesville, 1971).

[8] Stephen Booth, *An Essay on Shakespeare's Sonnets* (New Haven, 1969).

[9] Hermann Uhde-Bernays, "Catharina Regina von Greiffenberg: Ein Beitrag zur Geschichte des deutschen Lebens und Dichtens im 17. Jahrhundert" (Diss. Berlin, 1903); Leo Villiger, "Catharina Regina von Greiffenberg: Zu Sprache und Welt der barocken Dichterin" (Diss. Zürich, 1952).

[10] Malve Kristin Slocum, "Untersuchungen zu Lob und Spiel in den Sonetten der Catharina Regina von Greiffenberg" (Diss. Cornell, 1971).

[11] Horst Frank, "Catharina Regina von Greiffenberg: Untersuchungen zu ihrer Persönlichkeit und Sonettdichtung" (Diss. Hamburg, 1958); Peter Maurice Daly, "Die Metaphorik in den 'Sonetten' der Catharina Regina von Greiffenberg" (Diss. Zürich, 1964).

the poet's own disposition. He is able to demonstrate recurrent grammatical patterns and rhetorical formulas in the expression of certain dispositions in certain directions. He is less successful in persuading his reader that these are telling findings on the poems. It must be said in Frank's behalf that this second part of his dissertation has an air of forced labor about it. The first part is a careful and clearsighted biography of Catharina von Greiffenberg, based on the letters and other documents pertaining to her in the archives of the Pegnesischer Blumenorden in Nürnberg.[12] Daly classifies the metaphors of the sonnets according to the domain of their metaphoric terms (light, fire, water), according to the domain of their proper terms (God, man, faith), according to certain traits of style (*Dinglichkeit, Sprunghaftigkeit,* intensification), and according to grammatical type (vocative, appositive, demonstrative). No system of classification appears to have great bearing upon another, nor does the sum of these systems appear to have great bearing upon the poems. The value of the study is its clarification of the emblematic or mythic provenance of certain metaphors.

These three—the mainstream of German scholarship on the lyric poetry of the seventeenth century, another approach poorly represented in German scholarship and more at home in the British and American tradition, and the small corpus of work on Catharina von Greiffenberg—are a setting for my essay. I have tried to take a long, hard look at a small body of lyric poetry. I have looked to find the poem as a working construct, especially the sonnet as a working construct. I can lay no claim to a comprehensive treatment of Greiffenberg, having treated only the sonnets of her collection, and these under a specific aspect. The sonnets are open to examination under other aspects and the aspect I have used enjoys no exclusive legitimacy, though I have found it fruitful. I examine the sonnets for the way they are put together and for the bearing of one part upon another. Organization, it seems to me, is one of the most telling features of the sonnet. This is attributable in good part to the asymmetry of the sonnet, which affords relationships of great variety and great complexity among the parts of a poem. The complexity of these relationships can be traced also to the brevity of the sonnet. Because the form is brief, the elements which organize it occur in great density and their effect is intense.

I went in search of the organization of Greiffenberg's sonnets and found a variety of structural types, which I have arranged into a spectrum. The breadth of the spectrum and the fineness of its graduation have prompted me to speak of methods of composition in Greiffenberg's sonnets, for one can see from stage to stage just how the poems are constituted. The term is ambiguous and needs to be explained. I do not mean to describe the poet's process, but the poem's, and when I ascribe

---

[12] Published as Horst Frank, *Catharina Regina von Greiffenberg: Leben und Welt der barocken Dichterin* (Göttingen, 1967).

an effect in a poem to some effort of the poet, I do so as a convenience. My arrangement is a systematic construction—not a chronological reconstruction—of how these sonnets work. The simplest begin with two or four fine verses in which their initial impulse exhausts itself. They then proceed line by line to the completion of fourteen lines. The lines are succinct; their bearing on one another is tenuous and of little interest. These I have called linear sonnets. When the poet's control extends to full groups of lines, she composes sonnets with legitimate strophes. The relationship among these strophes is simple—typically one repeats another—and the sonnets are made up of discrete blocks. The poet uses devices of imagery or of thought which make the relationship among the strophes more intimate and more interesting. The linear sonnets and those made up of discrete blocks proceed on standard patterns: they repeat line by line or strophe by strophe, or one strophe expands upon another. In a fairly large group of sonnets the poet's control over the progress of a piece appears to break down altogether. The process of these poems I have called amassment, for they would seem to have been composed by introducing quantities of unformed material. Here is the turning point of my arrangement. There follows a group of sonnets composed neither by a standard procedure nor in the absence of all method. The poet is able to husband and exploit her resources of thought and material, to arrange her poem and control its progress. The sonnets at the end of the spectrum reflect a high order of control and poetic sovereignty, an integration of the poet's powers and her resources.

The systematic treatment of the sonnets touches at several points upon familiar problems of seventeenth-century poetry. Asyndeton, or more broadly, the Baroque catalogue, appears frequently in the linear poems, where I examine its possibilities in the sonnet. The poems of discrete blocks related by means of pictures illustrate how metaphor, simile, and allegory behave. In the poems composed without standard method, the poet encounters the larger and more difficult problems of her craft—the problems of disposing over idea and argument, of arrangement and final execution of a poem, of *dispositio* and *elocutio,* as they were called in contemporary poetics. Arrangement of the sonnets into a spectrum illustrates how she contends with these problems.

The organization of a sonnet is a subtle thing—ultimately a problem of interpretation and therefore a matter of demonstration and proof. Consequently, the search for the organization of these sonnets required that I attend to all manner of constituents of a poem. I consider the subjects of the poems, their material, and thought; their logic, rhetoric, and tone; their auditory qualities, rhythm, and diction; their syntax, punctuation and rhyme scheme—and these not in isolation, but always in their bearing upon one another. As this recitation shows, I have not found it possible to separate the poem as a text from the poem as a document in historical surroundings. The use of rhetorical forms and the attendant assumptions, the use of emblematic material and the attendant assumptions, the mythological, theological, and philosophic traditions of the time all belong to the context in which the sonnets are considered and all contribute to my attempt to interpret. Surely the old aesthetic problem which is stated as a dichotomy of literature as history and literature as art is a simplification for the sake of argument. I am not convinced of the primacy of either mode, and I suspect that allegiance to either extreme reduces our understanding of literature and our experience of it. Certainly the art of this particular literature, the seventeenth-century sonnet, is unintelligible without history. What we need is simultaneous vision, depth of field. If one is to address oneself to the one mode, then one ought to see it against the background of and in the context of the other.

While the systematic treatment of the sonnets is not exhaustive, it does explore fairly thoroughly how Catharina von Greiffenberg worked with a favored form. Some will believe my conclusions harsh, and I too am sure that my findings are not all incontestable. I hope that the process by which I arrived at them is always clear. For the sake of such clarity—for the sake of precision in observation, argument, and conclusion—I have restricted myself to these few sonnets and stated only what I have also tried to prove. The precision has a price, for painstaking presentation—especially of lyric poetry—makes for painstaking reading. Erich Trunz remarks laconically à propos of his exegeses of Gryphius' sonnets, "Sie lesen sich . . . immer schlecht."[13] The reader must work simultaneously with two texts, with the poetry and with the interpretation of the poetry, and he must mediate between the two when they seem to go their separate ways. He expends enormous energy on the multitude of minutiae which belong to precise and precisely argued interpretation. The whole enterprise can be called into question. On Shakespeare, C. S. Lewis concedes: "It is not contended that no man can enjoy the Sonnets without [such analysis] any more than that no man can enjoy a tune without knowing its musical grammar." But, Lewis continues, "unless we are content to talk simply about the 'magic' of Shakepeare's poetry (forgetting that magic was a highly formal art) something of the kind is inevitable."[14] I do not consider interpretation such as I have attempted here the ultimate use of poetry. I do believe that scrupulous interpretation is necessary if we are to understand these poems at their remove of three centuries, so that we can know them also in their immediacy as achievable experience. And I believe that utmost care in observation, combination, and presentation is necessary if we are not to continue to make silly statements and to copy one another's silly statements.

---

[13] Trunz, "Fünf Sonette," *Vom Geist der Dichtung,* p. 180.
[14] C. S. Lewis, *English Literature in the Sixteenth Century,* quoted by Booth, *Shakespeare's Sonnets,* p. 63.

The problem of organization in the sonnets belongs to the more complex problem of the poetic process itself, and my construction of how these poems are constituted gives account also of how one poet handles those constituents conveniently called idea, material, and form. The systematic arrangement of the sonnets explores how these raw resources are rendered into finished poetry, beginning with simple devices in the linear poems and concluding with sovereign control in the integrated sonnets. At every stage it is apparent that the poet is engaged in a balancing act and that an excess or insufficiency of any one element affects all. Greiffenberg's experience with these three defines itself more clearly when compared with Gryphius' in the next to last chapter of my essay, and the comparison permits some conclusions on the nature of Greiffenberg's powers. For example, the two poets differ significantly in their use of asyndeton and other forms of the catalogue. Greiffenberg's many linear sonnets would indicate that catalogues come about when her ideas fail to germinate and she fills the blank spaces of an incipient poem with new material, row upon row. In Gryphius' sonnets, on the other hand, idea grows to abundance, and the material in his catalogues is luminous with secondary meanings appropriate to the argument of the poem.

This aspect upon a common device of the lyric poetry of the period suggests the possibility of another aspect upon the poetry at large. Catalogues may well be a characteristic feature of Baroque poetry. But surely we are ready to go beyond this observation and ascertain that the figure performs utterly different functions from time to time. Only superficially is the catalogue in the first quatrain of Gryphius' "Menschliches Elende" ("Was sind wir Menschen doch . . .") an instance of "typische Aufweitung," as Conrady remarks (p. 229). To say that the figure represents a deictic attitude describes its function very broadly. And it dispenses much more than "dichterische Atmosphäre." The catalogue fairly bursts with secondary meanings which set forth the idea of transience in ever greater fullness. The insistence with which the catalogue urges its point is counterpart to the ineluctability of what it argues. Its loosening syntax corresponds to the dissolution it describes. When we see these figures not as forms apart, but each in its own setting and in conjunction with other components of that setting, our observation can be more discerning and our description more differentiated. Then Gryphius' catalogue appears not as an example of typical Baroque expansion but as an instance of a Baroque poet at work on a unique arrangement of specific material and its informing idea. As the comparison between Gryphius and Greiffenberg indicates, there are vast differences in the way contemporary poets attack such a problem.

It lies in the nature of the subject that my essay should explore not only the practices to which a sonnet lends itself but also the limits of these practices. For Greiffenberg's sonnets try the limits again and again, and in a great variety of ways. Such are the uses of a less than perfect poet: the poetry presents not only fully finished performance, but also attempts of many kinds in which the nuts and bolts of the poet's craft still show. Walter Benjamin used a more tactful metaphor: "Die Form selbst . . . deren Ausprägung bisweilen umgekehrt proportional zu der Vollendung einer Dichtung stehen kann, wird gerade an dem schmächtigen Leib der dürftigen Dichtung, als ihr Skelett gewissermaßen, augenfällig."[15] And so I apologize no further for inflicting also Catharina von Greiffenberg's poorer poems upon my reader.

Aside from specific findings, I would hope that my attempt can suggest something about the usefulness of a heuristic approach to the lyric poetry of the German Baroque. I have tried to develop a method both rigorous and inquisitive—neither intuitive or evocative at the one extreme nor pretentious to incontestible truth at the other, but intended to show certain features of these poets, of the lyric poetry of the period, and of the sonnet which might not have been seen in quite this fashion before.

---

[15] Walter Benjamin, *Ursprung des deutschen Trauerspiels*, rev. ed. (Frankfurt, 1963), p. 46.

CHAPTER TWO

GREIFFENBERG AND THE SONNETS

When the *Geistliche Sonnette* appeared in 1662, Catharina von Greiffenberg was twenty-eight.[1] She lived with her mother and her father's half brother, Hans Rudolf, who had become her guardian upon her father's death some twenty years earlier, in the familial castle Seysenegg, which her grandfather had acquired near Amstetten in Lower Austria shortly after he had been ennobled. The Greiffenbergs were Protestant. From this circumstance—convinced Protestantism in the midst of the Austrian Counter Reformation—Catharina's life and work gained its characteristic signature.

Catharina's central experience was her religion. All the efforts of her lifetime—the corpus of her works, her thoughts, even her friendships—were undertaken and carried out in the service of God. She had been dedicated before birth, when her mother had been dangerously ill, and at eighteen, in the aftermath of her younger sister's death, she experienced an illumination in the Protestant church at Pressburg, to which her family travelled regularly for worship. Henceforth she devoted her talents singlemindedly to the glory of God.

Her principal talent, for which she was unfailingly admired, was her fine intelligence. Her uncle had given her her early education, probably with elaborate care.[2] Catharina's natural inclination supplemented and complemented his efforts.[3] In her twenties she disposed over Latin and the three modern Romance languages; in her old age she learned Hebrew and Greek. She read massively. All her life she was given to seclusion: to reading, studying, contemplation—and to writing. This was her second great talent, and it, too, was given to the service of God.

Here again the circumstance of her life as a Protestant in the Austrian

---

[1] This description of Catharina's biography relies on Horst Frank, *Catharina Regina von Greiffenberg: Leben und Welt der barocken Dichterin* (Göttingen, 1967).

[2] Hans Rudolf was in love with his niece, even in her childhood and married her in 1664: Stubenberg to Birken, 13 November 1659; Birken to Caspar von Lilien, October 1663. These letters, and all others cited, are among Birken's papers in the Archiv des Pegnesischen Blumenordens, Germanisches Nationalmuseum, Nürnberg. Blake Lee Spahr's meticulous description of the Archive's holdings on Greiffenberg, *The Archives of the Pegnesischer Blumenorden* (Berkeley, 1960) pp. 38-50, greatly expedited my work there.

[3] Catharina's autodidacticism is cited repeatedly: Birken to Lilien, October 1663; Hans Rudolf to Birken, 5 June 1660; "Zuschrifft" to Catharina von Greiffenberg *Geistliche Sonnette / Lieder und Gedichte* (Nürnberg, 1662), p. [ix].

Counter Reformation was decisive, not only in that she chose to write religious pieces, but also in the literary influences—and the absence of literary influences—upon her work. The Protestants in Lower Austria were cut off from Austria's Catholic Baroque. The literary figures of this group—and they were numerous—looked to Nürnberg for the counsel and the society of likeminded literati, and here they published their translations and their verse epics. Such a man was Johann von Stubenberg.[4]

Stubenberg, whose castle Schallaburg lay not far from Seysenegg, was a Baroque literary dilettante par excellence. He translated tirelessly from Italian, French, and Latin. He moved in a vast circle of literary acquaintances, especially in Lower Austria, brought them into contact with one another, and sponsored their petitions for membership in the Fruchtbringende Gesellschaft, to which he belonged. He enjoyed the personal friendship of Harsdörffer and Birken. Stubenberg was Catharina's literary mentor. He advised her on her reading. Probably he encouraged her to practice exercises in poetry.[5] Certainly he emended her early poems and taught her the rules of poetics.[6] From him Catharina may have learned of the Nürnbergers' practice of rich rhyme and auditory effect; the technique became characteristic of her poetry.

Nevertheless, Catharina wrote in relative isolation. Though there may have been many minor literary figures among the Austrian Protestants, she worked closely only with Stubenberg. She belonged to no school, and her sonnets have escaped the normalizing effects of poetizing as a form of social intercourse. The poems are distinctively, even peculiarly, her own. Furthermore, her early poems[7] were essentially a private production: Catharina composed them out of and recorded them into her religious experience, which at this time was still purely private. Her religion imbued all her activities—her reading and study, her thought, which may already have taken the form of contemplative devotionals,[8] and her translation[9] and writing—and all these activities were carried out in seclusion. Only later, when she had become a public literary figure, does she appear to have written with the thought that she might be read, and then she wrote, not simply poems, but devotionals in which poems appeared among prose explications of and reflections on biblical

---

[4] Martin Bircher, *Johann Wilhelm von Stubenberg und sein Freundeskreis* (Berlin, 1968), describes the literary landscape of Lower Austria in the seventeenth century and Stubenberg's relationship to Catharina at length. See especially pp. 198-204.

[5] Bircher, p. 201, conjectures reasonably that the epigrams appended to the sonnets are poetic exercises in which Stubenberg may have encouraged Catharina.

[6] Stubenberg to Birken, 13 November 1659 (see below, p. 11).

[7] The sonnets in the collection were probably composed between 1655 and 1660: see below, p. 15 n. 24.

[8] Frank, pp. 91, 95, describes Catharina's personal devotionals.

[9] In the course of 1660 she translated du Bartas' *Triomphe de la foy*, published as *Der Glaubens-Triumf* in an appendix to *Sieges-Seule der Buße und Glaubens / wider den Erbfeind Christlichen Namens* (1675).

passages.[10] Finally, as her devotional books, her sole production in later life, demonstrate, Catharina, whose primary calling was to the service of God, never saw herself as a professional poet. She remained an amateur, and this absence of professionalism has left its mark on her collection of sonnets. It is only reasonable to assume, from the nature of these first poems[11] as well as from the circumstances under which Catharina wrote them—as a young, unmarried woman in rural Austria, a Protestant among Catholics—that at the time of their composition she did not intend them for publication.

And yet they were published. In the fall of 1659 Stubenberg sent a copy of one of Catharina's sonnets[12] to Birken. Birken apparently was impressed, for Stubenberg responded to his friend's interest in Catharina by describing her in his letter of 13 November 1659:

> Betr. dz Fraülein v. Greiffenberg, deren Sonnett dem Erwachßenem so wohlgefällig, ist Mir nicht allein Vertraülich bekannt, sondern Meine halbe Schulerinn gewesen, Zu Seisenekk in Oesterreich 4 Meilen von Mir wohnhafft, dahero Ich vilmahls die Ehre gehabt daß Sie Mir ihre sachen anfangs Zuverbessern übersändet, anjezt aber ist die Schulerinn über den Meister. Sie hatt dem Röm. Keyser eine Krone Reichsstab, Schwertt, Apfel u. Adler fast lebensgroß von lauter Versen gemacht,[13] die Ich wündschte daß d. H. sehen möchte. Sie hatt ihre einige lust am lesen ist d. Französisch- und Welschen Sprache kundig, auch in etwas der Hispanischen. . . .

There the matter rested until the spring of 1660, when Stubenberg, again apparently in response to an inquiry from Birken, mentioned Catharina once more. This letter is dated 6 April 1660. On 9 April, Hans Rudolf wrote to Birken:

> Mein Ser-Groser Freint Herr Hanns Wilhelbm, Herr v. Stubenberg, hat mihr . . . ain Zedel von Meines Herrn Hant heitt Ÿbershikht, daraus Ih VerNumben dz Mein Herr Ain Sonnet Gesöhen . . . Wölhes Mein Herr, Herr v. Stubenberg Neben Ainem Zwar Vnuertienten Grossen lob ÿberSentet. . . . ob Ih Nun Wohl die öhr Meines Herrn Khuntschaft Anders Niht Als durh dessen heraus khumme Raumbwiertige Shriften habe, So Vnter Stehe Ih Mih doh

---

[10] An exception to the devotional books is the *Sieges-Seule*, an epic in alexandrines begun in 1663, which Frank, pp. 50-51, describes as "in seinem umfangreichsten Teil eine auf sorgfältigen historischen Studien fußende Geschichte des Islam und seiner Auseinandersetzung mit dem Christentum, angefangen von Mohammed. . . . [Die Dichterin] entwickelt die Geschichte des Islam in seiner Auseinandersetzung mit den christlichen Völkern als die Geschichte des Bösen in seinem irdischen Kampf gegen den heiligen Glauben." Obviously the piece was intended for public consumption: it was a sustained project of topical interest. Catharina began work on it after the appearance of the sonnets.
[11] See below, pp. 16-17.
[12] As Spahr, *Archives*, p. 47, and Frank, *Greiffenberg*, p. 149 n. 128, have pointed out independently, the poem must be sonnet 47 in the collection.
[13] These pattern poems have been lost: Frank, p. 31.

dem selbigen Edlihe Sonnet, von Ihrer Erfintung Vnt Aingenen Hant Shrift Zu V̇bersenten, Mit dienstliher Pitte, Solhe ZuerSöhen, Vnt Mihr dessen Vrthail Vnt Mainung V̇ber Solhe Durh ain Prieffl an Mih Zuertheillen V. Zu V̇bershreiben. So es etwa Nit Gar Aine Grosse VerMessenhait Were[,] Wurten Sih Alberait der getihte Von Ihr auffgesözt *Maiste Gaistlihe*, Aine Zimblihe anZahl beFinten, die Wolte Ih *Vnter Meinen Namben, Mit* Vermelten, dz Sie Solhe Zwar auffgesözt, *Ih* Aber *an Ihre Erlaubnus* dieselbigen *Ihr Zu öhr Vnt Getöhtnus trukhen lassen,* heraus Geben, doh Vorhero Mein Herrn Vmb dessen hohVerstentige *Corectur* Pitten[.] Ih VerMeinte, dieweil Solhe *durh Ain Weibs Pershon* Auffgesözt, Möhte Selbige, *desto Angenember* Sein, In deme dergleihen V̇bungen Nah der Zeit Pey dissem Weiblihen Geshlöhte nit So Gar geMeine. ... Pitte Also Mein Herr Mihr Vnd besagter Meiner Freiln Maumb die öhr Zu thauen Vnt Mih dessen WolMeinen V. Getruen Raht hieriber Zu Wiertigen[.]

The poems which Hans Rudolf enclosed also found favor with Birken. On 5 June 1660 Hans Rudolf wrote a second letter, replying to Birken's of 25 April.[14] He thanks Birken for his "höfflihes erpieten" and continues:

... auff Meines Herrn Guetahten, wil Ih die Edlihe [in the margin: Auff 300] Sonet V. Antere Getiht Zusamb ortnen, Vnt *Vnter Meinem Namben*, doh mit ainer *Vertrukhten Erinerung*, herausgeben, dz Sie Solhe Auffgesözt, V. Ih Ihr Zu öhren gleihwohl *ane Ihr wissen* Solhe habe In trukh geben[.] Mit *Hern Enter* hab Ih Geret, der Wil Solhes *auff Seinm aigenen Vnkosten* [?] *trukhen* V. werte Ih Ihme Auff Negst khumbet *Bartolome*, dz Werkhl Zu linz V̇berantworten. ...

Hans Rudolf reminded Birken that he wanted him "*die Corectur* des Werkh auff Sih Zu Nemben, Vnt Auh was etwa hin Vnd her Fölet oder In der Khunst Versözt Ist *Zu VerPessern.*" He asked Birken to honor the work with a sonnet and to obtain for it "Ain oder Zwee berimbte: Ja Raih. Worte";[15] he himself would yet forward such a testimony from Stubenberg. The letter concludes: "Pitte Alßo Nohmahlen Mein Herr wolle Als Ain *Vatter der tihtKhunst,* Vns, Nemblih Mih V. disse Mein Freiln Maumb Als Ain Shulerin In Solher lassen befolhen Sein, Vnt deren Feller In disser Khunst, Mit Vätterlihen Wohlgeneigten Gemiet bedökhen."

The poems, then, were sent to Birken from Linz on Bartholomew's Day 1660. They were published by Michael Endter, Nürnberg, in the spring of 1662. The title page, the "Vertrukhte Erinerung" which Hans Rudolf had requested, is followed by a long preface over Hans Rudolf's

[14] The letter is lost.
[15] Birken tried unsuccessfully to obtain poems from Neumark, Schottel, Rist, and Moscherosch: Bircher, p. 203. The sonnets appeared with accompanying poems by Birken, Stubenberg, Wolfgang Helmhard von Hohberg, and Jakob Sturm. The two latter belonged to Stubenberg's circle of acquaintances.

name,[16] in which Catharina's biography is briefly told, her love of God, virtue, and learning extolled, and the assurance advanced: ". . . ich habe mich erkühnet / ohne meiner geliebten Fräul. Muhme Vorwissen und Erlaubniß / eine Anzahl derselben [the poems] in den Druck färtigen zu lassen . . . nicht zweifflend . . . meine geliebte Fräul. Muhm werde mir solches / da es etwan wider ihren Willen geschehen / nicht verargen können."[17] Ostensibly the idea of publishing the poems originated in Hans Rudolf. He collected them, arranged them, and sent them to Birken, who edited them and sponsored their publication.[18] All this happened without Catharina's knowledge.

The story is not probable, and none of Catharina's biographers gives it much credence.[19] In all likelihood, Catharina not only knew of the plan to publish the poems, but also cooperated in it. The question of her knowledge is easily answered: she would hardly have failed to observe that Hans Rudolf removed a manuscript of more than three hundred poems from the house. Her awareness of the project has other ramifications: the plan to have Birken publish the poems probably originated not in Hans Rudolf but in Stubenberg. Benevolence toward literary friends was Stubenberg's habit. He knew Catharina's poems; in his capacity as a connoisseur he recognized their quality. Hans Rudolf, for all his love for and admiration of his niece, was no lover of literature, as the style and the orthography of his letters amply testify. Stubenberg alone could have supplied the link between Hans Rudolf and Birken, who were unacquainted with one another. Furthermore, when Hans Rudolf wrote Birken on 9 April 1660, the day he received Birken's letter from Stubenberg, the plan had already been worked out in detail. Birken was to correct the poems; they were to appear under Hans Rudolf's name. It seems likely that the plan had evolved over the previous winter, between Birken's warm reaction to the first sample of Catharina's sonnets in November and his second inquiry about her in April, and that in this second inquiry Stubenberg and Hans Rudolf saw

---

[16] That he actually wrote this preface is more than dubious. A comparison of its literary quality to that of Hans Rudolf's letters indicates as much. Bircher, p. 202, quotes Stubenberg in a letter to Birken, 12 September 1661: "wegen des H. v. *Greiffenbergs* vorrede habe Jch Mich mit dem *Sinnreichem* [Hohberg] unterredt, u. befunden, daß es nicht tuhlich, selbigem derer änderung zuzumuhten, dann, könnte Er es besser machen, hätte er es ohne Zweyfel getahn. . . ."

[17] "Zuschrifft" to the *Geistliche Sonnette,* pp. [x]-[xi].

[18] Birken furnished the volume with an emblematic etching and an explanatory poem, a poem in Catharina's honor, and a long "Vor-Ansprache," in the main an apologia for a female author. See Frank, pp. 34-35.

[19] Leo Villiger, "Catharina Regina von Greiffenberg: Zu Sprache und Welt der barocken Dichterin" (Diss. Zürich, 1952), p. 19, construes the assurance that Catharina knew nothing of the publication as a formula to cover "die Zurückhaltung der Frau vor einem selbständigen Auftreten"; Frank, p. 34, finds the assurance questionable, but assumes that Catharina took no part in the preparation of the manuscript; Bircher does not treat the problem.

an opportunity to launch the project. In neither of his preliminary letters to Birken does Hans Rudolf say that Catharina does not know of the plan to publish her poems. He says only that the projected volume should give notice of her ignorance, and in his first letter he states his reason clearly: a woman's publishing her own original poems might give offense. Finally, though this point cannot be pressed, at the conclusion of his second letter Hans Rudolf commends both himself and his niece to Birken's tutelage and benevolence. It is safe to conclude that Catharina knew of the project, probably from its inception. It was Stubenberg's plan, and he had no reason to conceal it from her—quite the contrary.

The question of Catharina's participation in the undertaking is more difficult. Before the manuscript could be sent to Birken, the poems which were to be published had to be selected and arranged in sequence. Conceivably the poems were never subjected to a rigorous selection. The published collection's remarkable range of quality—from simple exercises to finished sonnets, and in the sonnets alone from the extremely primitive to the highly sophisticated[20]—suggests that the poems were not scrupulously culled. Their very number—250 sonnets plus fifty-two *Lieder*, interspersed with again forty-eight other pieces, when the poet was not yet thirty years old—contributes to this conjecture. Nevertheless, the collection does not represent Catharina's entire production to date. In 1654 an anonymous sonnet, probably Catharina's,[21] appeared as a tribute to Stubenberg in his translation of Bacon's *Sermones Fideles*. In both conception and technique it is markedly more callow than the sonnets published in 1662. At some point, then, there must have been a selection, whether during the preparation of the manuscript or simply in Catharina's private filing system. It is unlikely that Hans Rudolf's literary accomplishment was commensurate to such a task.

There remains the problem of arrangement. The sequence of the sonnets has troubled all of Catharina's critics.[22] Tellingly, however, no one

[20] See below, p. 23.

[21] Martin Bircher and Peter M. Daly, "Catharina Regina von Greiffenberg und Johann Wilhelm von Stubenberg: Zur Frage der Autorschaft zweier anonymer Widmungsgedichte," *Literaturwissenschaftliches Jahrbuch der Görres Gesellschaft*, 7 (1966), 17-35. The poem in question appears as the frontispiece and on p. 27.

[22] Villiger, p. 19, refutes the analysis by Hermann Uhde-Bernays, "Catharina Regina von Greiffenberg: Ein Beitrag zur Geschichte des deutschen Lebens und Dichtens im 17. Jahrhundert" (Diss. Berlin, 1903), but his own makes such fine distinctions that it loses coherence; Frank, *Greiffenberg*, p. 34, finds the sequence unsatisfactory in its arbitrary schematism, which he attributes to Hans Rudolf. In his dissertation "Catharina Regina von Greiffenberg: Untersuchungen zu ihrer Persönlichkeit und Sonettdichtung" (Hamburg, 1958), pp. 146-47, he offers a breakdown which is largely consonant with, though more detailed than, my own. John H. Sullivan, "The German Religious Sonnet in the Seventeenth Century," (Diss. Berkeley, 1966), pp. 202-07, alone takes no exception to the published arrangement. His description of the groups of poems, especially of those in the second half of the collection, is similar to mine, though he, too, breaks the poems more finely.

who has ever written on Catharina has attempted to rearrange the sonnets or even to emend the present arrangement. The reason is obvious: the poems do not lend themselves to any other arrangement. To be sure, there are flaws in their sequence, poems which appear where they should not,[23] but seen at large, and particularly with reference to the poems' potential for arrangement, the present sequence is altogether satisfactory. The 250 sonnets are not a cycle, nor are they a series of cycles. They are not a closed composition of any kind, and they cannot be arranged into a closed composition, simply because they were not written as such. The poems were written at random over a number of years[24] and never intended for collection and publication. Under these circumstances, their present arrangement appears reasonable, even felicitous.

Not only are the groups into which the sonnets are arranged fairly homogeneous,[25] but the groups themselves relate to one another. The sonnets are broken into hundreds, and broken again into smaller groups on a given topic. Thus the volume begins with ten poems on praising God (*Lob*), which Catharina saw as her essential task in the service of God;[26] these are followed by a group on God's miraculous governance (*Wunderregierung*); then by poems which petition God's help in a certain undertaking (*Vorhaben*);[27] and finally by a large group on adversity (*Unglück*), which itself breaks into reflections on the essential nature of adversity, consolation in adversity, and joy upon emergence from adversity. The second hundred are three-quarters given over to a life of Christ from birth to ascension and turn then to holy communion, from which reflections on Pentecost and the inspiration of the Holy Spirit proceed; poems on the Trinity follow naturally. The final fifty begin with a group of twenty poems which are truly miscellaneous. These are succeeded by sonnets on the four seasons beginning with winter and concluding with autumn, and the volume ends with poems on the eternal life.

[23] Notably sonnets 245 and 246 in the midst of a concluding group on the eternal life.

[24] Bircher, p. 200, conjectures that the poems were written largely between 1655 and 1660. The assumption is reasonable, particularly in the light of the contrast between the anonymous sonnet of 1654 and the sonnets in the 1662 collection.

[25] This matter should not be pressed: a given sonnet does not stand in any necessary or unalterable relationship to its predecessor or successor, but then again, it seldom clashes with them. The source of Villiger's and Frank's dissatisfaction with the arrangement may have been their inclination to see its particulars rather than to be content with its general fabric.

[26] The point is made several times in the poems, notably in sonnets 6 and 9 and in Lied 24. See also Frank, "Greiffenberg" (Diss.), pp. 117-19.

[27] This "undertaking" is never clearly described. Frank, passim and especially pp. 73-87, has reconstructed Catharina's personal mission: nothing less than the religious conversion of the imperial house of Austria. The mission became visible only later in her life. Nevertheless, there are veiled references to something outside the poem in several sonnets, notably in sonnet 34, lines 10-11 and 13; sonnet 36, lines 10-11 and 13; sonnet 47, lines 13-14; sonnet 67 passim; sonnet 70, line 14; sonnet 201, lines 10-14; sonnet 210, lines 9-12.

The collection begins with poems of praise, the quintessence of Catharina's mission on earth, and concludes with the beyond; in the first hundred the person of the poet is prominent; the second hundred has Christian history and the Christian sacraments as its object; to the final fifty are relegated the miscellaneous and "secular" poems (though they, too, are essentially religious). Each hundred culminates at its conclusion: the first in a burst of joy after tribulation; the second in poems on the Trinity, the most esoteric of the Christian dogmas; and the final fifty with eternity, the obvious conclusion for such a volume. The poems were arranged by someone who understood them and understood Catharina's religious experience well. Very well: sonnets 76 to 81, in the group on consolation in adversity, are a genuine cycle. The first sonnet is entitled "Uber ein zu ruck gegangenes / doch Christlich- und heiliges Vornemen"; Lied XXIII, entitled "Auf die in den Sonneten gedachte zuruckgegangene Pfingst-Reise," makes clear that this Christian intention was a trip to a Protestant church, perhaps in Pressburg, for worship. In these six sonnets the poet reacts to the thwarted trip: she expresses her defiance of this adversity (76); quarrels with God and then reconciles herself with his mysterious ways (77); repents of her defiance and submits to God's rule (78); reinterprets the experience to her advantage (79); describes the advantage she will gain explicitly (80); and generalizes the advantage into a belief in God's abiding solicitude for her (81).[28] Only Catharina held the key to these poems. Doubtless she arranged them; in all likelihood she arranged the entire collection.

The *Geistliche Sonnette,* then, are a collection of poems written by a devout woman in her mid-twenties. They were written at random: that is to say, they are the precipitate of the religious experience which informed the poet's entire biography, and their composition was adjunct to this experience. Catharina was an amateur, and her amateurishness has had both a salutary and a deleterious effect upon the quality of her published collection. The poems were not published at the poet's behest. The plan probably came from Stubenberg, who moved in literary circles and had seen his own books appear. Catharina, however, knew of this plan, and it stands to reason, in keeping both with human nature and with circumstantial evidence, that she cooperated in it. If the published poems represent a selection from her entire production, and if the poems have been arranged knowledgeably, then probability alone indicates that Catharina selected and arranged them. The *Geistliche Sonnette* are the genuine document of a gifted amateur.

The collection bears this mark. Not a few of the poems have their raison d'être only in the private realm of Catharina's personal religious experience; they read like diary entries cast into a special form (that of the sonnet). There are sonnets in which the poet's thoughts simply fix on one point and circumscribe it again and again, as if in the disciplined

---

[28] For discussion of sonnets 76 and 78 see below, pp. 61-64 and pp. 78-80.

contemplation of a devotional exercise. In other poems the thought moves freely—to use a pejorative expression: aimlessly—from one point to another, as if in free meditation. In a very large number of sonnets the initial literary impulse is exhausted at the end of the first four lines, or even the first two, and the remainder of the poem has been forced together by one method or another, or even in the absence of all method, until the final product contains fourteen lines, if little else. Other poems lack even felicitous opening lines and appear to have been undertaken in the absence of any impulse at all. The explanation is that writing a poem was for the poet also a religious observance, that the impulse to these pieces lay outside the realm of literature and poetry in Catharina's obligations to God. Yet for all the primacy of her religion, Catharina was and remains a poet. The collection contains abysmal poems; it also contains superb ones. The range of its quality is another mark of the amateur.

According to their organization, Greiffenberg's sonnets fall into three groups: the *linear* poems, which accumulate line by line; the poems made up of succinct and relatively independent strophes, of *discrete* blocks; and the sonnets whose strophes are *integrated*. The linear poems are the simplest. Though their lines tend to form groups of four, these groups are little more than a succession of lines, and the poems themselves are little more than a succession of lines. There are no genuine strophes. Sonnet 75 is an example:[29]

75
Uber Gottes Wunderführung.

DU wunder Heiligkeit / und Heilig hohes Wunder!
du machest alles wol / und siht doch selzam aus.
Offt / wann du segnen wilst / komt erst ein starker Strauß.
Wann Hülff' erscheinen soll / geh'n offt die Mittel unter.
   Es fället offt in Brunn der helle Hoffnung Zunder.
Entgegen gibt die See / ein Fünklein offt heraus.
Voll wunder-Liechter ist / GOtt / dein vorsehungs Hauß.
Dein' Obacht ist auf uns / mit stäten Sorgen / munder.
   Die Insul ist bereit / eh man zu Schiffe geht /
wo nach dem Schiffbruch uns das Meer pflegt auszuwerffen.
Von dem / den du beschützst / der Wind die Kugeln weht.
   nicht weiter / als du schaffst / die Blitz' hin blicken dörffen.
Du lenkest alle Ding' / und übergiebst den Sieg
Dem Glauben / daß ihm / dir zu Ehren / alls erlieg.

The subject of the poem (and of the two which will follow) is God's miraculous governance. After an appropriate address, the second line

---

[29] The texts of all the sonnets reproduced here are taken from the copy of Greiffenberg's *Geistliche Sonnette / Lieder und Gedichte* (Nürnberg, 1662) in the von Faber du Faur Collection of the Beinecke Library, Yale University. There are a few linguistic obscurities in the poem. "Strauß" = strife (line 3); "blicken" = *blitzen* (line 11).

states the poem's thesis: despite appearances, God rectifies all things. The motif appears in many sonnets. God's mysterious way, this contrast between semblance and ultimate reality, is for Greiffenberg the essence of the miraculous. After stating its thesis, the poem moves into a series of examples to bear out the point. The poem in fact consists in these examples, line upon line, and the succession runs through a third quatrain. Here the focus changes slightly: taking her departure from the statement on God's solicitude in line 8, the poet speaks not only of impersonal forces in nature, but also of God's protective intervention. The shift leads directly into the conclusion, which begins in line 13. Nevertheless these instances are also cited line by line, and the alternating rhyme deprives the strophe of whatever cohesion the embracing rhyme of the first two strophes may have effected. Minor variations in the process of linear accumulation—the juxtaposition of converse examples in lines 5 and 6, the general observations which interrupt the flow of examples in lines 7 and 8, or the two-line example at the beginning of the third quatrain—are not sufficient to overcome the tedium of which the fourfold recurrence of "offt" in lines 3-6 is symptomatic.

A conclusion for such a poem is inevitably a difficulty, for a list, unlike a column of figures, cannot be reduced to a simple sum without loss. Here four words of summation suffice: "Du lenkest alle Ding'." The rest is an extraneous point introduced abruptly and left undeveloped: the power of faith in God's governance and, parenthetically, faith's contribution to God's glory—topics which are prominent in the poet's repertory and which find their proper treatment in other poems.

The sonnet, then, is made up of a two-line introduction in which it states its thesis, a series of examples to demonstrate the thesis, and a two-line conclusion, three quarters of it being only obliquely relevant. As the first halfline of the conclusion betrays, the problem under consideration is no more highly developed at the end of the piece than at the beginning. The poem consists of unexploited material accumulated in an orderly fashion, line by line.

The sonnets composed of discrete blocks constitute the largest of the three groups. At their simplest, they too are basically items in series, which, however, have been developed or enlarged to fill whole strophes. At their most sophisticated, they reflect a management of form and expression which reaches full development in the third group of poems, the integrated sonnets. Sonnet 61 is one of the simpler poems.

61
Uber Gottes regirende Wunderweise.

    DU wunder würker / soll dir was unmüglich fallen?
bey dir auch keines wegs die wunder wunder seyn!
voll unerhörter ding' / ist deiner Allmacht schrein /
die sich erweist und preist unendlich hoch in Allen.
    Da / wo die Sonne sitzt / entdecken sich die strahlen:

> wo GOtt ist / siehet man der wunder reinen schein /
> die ihm / wie uns das gehn / sind eigen und gemein.
> in ihm sie / voll begierd uns zugefallen / wallen.
>   Der Glaubens-Donner bricht die Wolken / daß der blitz /
> die Göttlich Herrlichkeit / in werken sich entdecket /
> gezeugt aus trübsals kält' und Menschen-Liebehitz.
>   Gott / zu erquicken / offt uns eine Angst erwecket.
> In Unglücks Abgrund hat sein Höh-Art ihren sitz:
> das süß auf bitterkeit / und Freud' auf Leid / wol schmecket.

Instead of stating its thesis flatly in a single line, like sonnet 75, the poem poses a rhetorical question after the initial halfline address and answers the question in line 2, elaborating and emphasizing the response in the following sentence. The process requires four lines: the sonnet begins with a genuine strophe, even though the relative clause in line 4 is superfluous and vague.

The second quatrain does not really follow from the first. The illustration which it presents and then explains follows from line 3, but line 4 has diverted the progress of the discourse, so that the second strophe must make a new beginning. The illustration is well chosen, not only in the validity of the analogy between the sun and its rays on the one hand and God and his miracles on the other, but also in the congruence between God and the sun (brilliance, majesty, power, and altitude), and between the rays and the miracles, which are themselves described as "reiner schein." The relative clause in line 7 underscores the basic analogy of the comparison in lines 5-6 tellingly and with an endearing absence of pomposity. In this strophe, too, however, the final line is something less than entirely successful. The abundance of God's miraculous goodness could proceed convincingly from the discussion of God and the sun, which is also abundant, but here, after the relative clause on an entirely different aspect of the analogy, the statement seems appended.

The first tercet takes up a new problem and thus is separate and removed from the foregoing. The power of faith is represented in a short allegory, at first dense in the compound "Glaubens-Donner" and then extended in the participial modifier (line 11). "Glaubens-Donner" is a purely functional metaphor: faith and thunder are similar only insofar as they both break the clouds, themselves representative simultaneously of the meteorological phenomenon and of a spiritual state. Lightning and God's grandeur are equated by apposition. To this point the allegory is tight and compact—full of implications at no great expense of words. In line 11 it becomes thin and wordy. The role of heat and cold in the production of the natural phenomenon is clear, as is the equation of distress with chill and love with warmth, but the function of distress and love in the production of the spiritual event is less perspicuous and therefore more strained.

The second tercet takes up another facet in the complex of God's miraculous governance. It associates from "trübsals kält" in line 11 to "Angst" in line 12 under the common aspect adversity and introduces a contrast between semblance and ultimate reality, treated at length in sonnet 75. There is a problem here of cohesion within the strophe. Line 12 is a syntactically self-sufficient aphorism. It is followed by two instances of its truth. These are materially diverse, for line 13 plots the abyss against the height, while line 14 speaks of sweetness and bitterness, of joy and sorrow. Only the logic of the lines and the syntactical dependence of line 14 upon line 13 bind them.

The strophes of the poem are genuine. They are not merely the result of syntactical or rhythmical breaks between lines, but genuine units of composition within which thought unfolds. These units, however, are relatively independent of one another. The two quatrains spring from one thought, but they become separated when the last line of the first quatrain diverts the progress of this thought. Each of the tercets handles a new thought. The poem breaks into discrete blocks.

The sonnet deteriorates steadily. The quatrains are almost continuous; the focus of the first tercet is new and of small relevance to the foregoing; the second tercet, which again changes the focus, suffers from fragile internal connections. The poem also deteriorates periodically—at the end of each strophe. Line 4 makes the quatrains disjunctive; line 8 is appended to the second quatrain after the discourse has moved away from God's bounty; line 11 laboriously extends the first tercet's allegory; the quality of the whole second tercet is dubious. The poet is unable to sustain the discourse. Toward the end of each strophe the topic under discussion is exhausted. Hence the leap to another topic and a fresh impetus; hence also the strophes' strained last lines; and hence the general exhaustion at the end of the piece. The sonnet treats only disjointed aspects of a larger complex.

An integrated sonnet consists of a continuous discussion projected over more than one strophe. It is organized in such a fashion that a strophe proceeds effortlessly from its predecessor and builds upon it. At their best, integrated sonnets are controlled formal and logical constructs in which no word is wasted. When the method, the idea, and the material of such a poem are all implicit in one another, the effect is superb.

Sonnet 60, a less than perfect poem, illustrates the necessary organization of the argument.

60
[Auf das verwirrte widerwärtige aussehen.]

GLäub / wann du schon nit sihst / den der kan müglich machen
die selbst' unmüglichkeit / bey welchem Sonnen-Liecht
dein dunkles schicksel ist. Die ausgangs-schnur Er flicht
in dem zerrütten Strenn so seltner sinnen-sachen.

Er giebet nach / und dreht den Faden bey den schwachen /

> wie sehr verhenkt und klenkt er ist / ihn doch nicht bricht /
> am Glückes-Haspel / mit der zeit / ihn recht ausricht.
> Sein fleiß und weißheit pflegt (schläfft lust und Glück) zu wachen.
> Denk nicht / daß ihm / wie dir / das mittel sey verdeckt.
> Sein Allsicht-Aug durchtringt die undurchdringlichkeiten
> der heimlichkeit geheim / im wunder-Berg versteckt.
> Sein' Allmachts hitz / den Stahl zu lob-Gold kan bereiten.
> Sein' Ehr' hat ihr in ihr ein Ehren-ärz erweckt /
> das wird mit seinem Bild sich in die Welt ausbreiten.

The structural supports of the poem are the imperatives at the beginning of the octave and the beginning of the sestet. These each carry over into a description of God's governance, which is the subject of the poem. The first imperative entails two relative clauses which attribute to God those powers from which his governance, as it is described here, proceeds. These clauses are, as it were, an index to the poem's contents. In the first clause the play on "müglich machen . . . unmüglichkeit" redoubles the sense of God's power, making him omnipotent. The effect is heightened in "selbst' unmüglichkeit," where "selbst'" has the position and the punctuation and thus analogically the function of an attributive adjective—in the superlative degree.[30] The second clause plots "Sonnen-Liecht" against "dunkles schicksel," a simple, unaffected turn of phrase which makes it possible to implicate both relative clauses in the following sentence.

The second sentence's point of departure is God's omnipotence, attributed to him in the first relative clause. This power is exercised in spinning (or plaiting) a thread, an "ausgangs-schnur." The reference is probably to Ariadne.[31] The exit here is from a frayed skein ("zerrütter Strenn" = *Strähne*) which is equated by means of genitive identification with "seltne sinnen-sachen." A "sinnen-sache" must be a puzzle:[32] on the one hand a labyrinth, implied by "ausgangs-schnur," on the other hand "dunkles schicksel," implied by the pointing formula [33] "*so* seltner sinnen-sachen." Thus not only is dark destiny sunlight in God's eyes; also obscure destiny is a labyrinthine puzzle from which God, in his omnipotence and omniscience, can find a way out.

---

[30] *Selbst* appears in the same usage and fully inflected in several sonnets. Its adjectival function and its meaning are unambiguous in sonnet 217, line 6: "Es ist das selbs*te* Gut nicht gut."

[31] "Ausgangs-schnur" also echoes Psalm 19, which speaks, tóo, of the sun (line 2) and of the glory of God ("Ehre," line 13): "Die Himmel erzählen die Ehre Gottes, und die Feste verkündigt seiner Hände Werk. . . . Ihre Schnur geht aus in alle Lande und ihre Rede an der Welt Ende. Er hat der Sonne eine Hütte an ihnen gemacht" (Psalm 19, 1 and 5). Despite these coincidences, I have not been able to reconcile the words in the sonnet with the sense of the Psalm.

[32] Something about which one puzzles. To puzzle about something = *darüber sinnen*. Implicit also in *Sinnen-Bild* = *Emblem*. See Dietrich Walter Jöns, *Das "Sinnen-Bild": Studien zur allegorischen Bildlichkeit bei Andreas Gryphius* (Stuttgart, 1966), p. 3.

[33] Christine Brooke-Rose, *A Grammar of Metaphor*, 2nd ed. (London, 1965), p. 69.

The thread in God's hands associates the second quatrain with the first, but here the thread is no longer Ariadne's but Clotho's, a transformation already prepared in the equation "dunkles schicksel" = "sinnen-sachen" = "zerrütter Strenn." An allegory ensues in which God spins the thread, handling it gently because it is tangled ("verhenkt und klenkt"),[34] and finally arranges it "am Glückes-Haspel," which could mean the reel simply of fortune or of good fortune. The implication in either case is God's benevolence. In the final line of this quatrain the poem first becomes thin. As in the last two lines of sonnet 61, opposite qualities, sleeping and waking, are plotted against one another. The tension between the two verbs is spurious, for "schlafen" here means "to be absent"; its English equivalent is "dormant" in figurative usage. In this context it is no real antonym to "wachen."

The poem recovers promptly from this lapse. The second imperative, like the first a strong piling which can support a long span, reaches backward to the second relative clause at the outset of the poem, in which also God's powers of vision are described. Supported on these two pilings, the poem has a continuous sweep. In lines 10 and 11 the etymological reinforcement of meaning is even more intense than in the poem's first two lines. "Durchtringt die undurchdringlichkeiten" is analogous to "müglich machen . . . unmüglichkeit." "Heimlichkeit" is redoubled not only in "geheim," but again in "versteckt," and once more, though not etymologically, in "wunder-Berg," the magic mountain, archetypal locus of secrets and mysteries, particularly of divine secrets. "Allsicht-Aug" is the converse of "selbst' unmüglichkeit." Here normal adjectival usage is discarded in favor of a noun compounded with another. The quality of all-seeingness is not merely attributed to God's eye; rather all-sight itself and the eye become constituents of a larger whole.

Then the carefully managed continuity of the poem is at an end. The second tercet is connected to the foregoing neither formally, like the first tercet, nor materially, like the second quatrain. Whatever link may be effected by the word "Allmacht," which would associate the strophe with the first relative clause, is tenuous as the word fairly disappears in a long, complicated metaphor to which it is peripheral. The metaphor, in which heat transforms steel into gold, refers not only to the alchemy of gaining a precious metal from a common and, in the manufacture of weapons, cruel one, but also, implicitly, to the four ages of man in the Astrea legend.[35] An era of hardship is transformed into a more favorable age. In line 13, the first "ihr" is the reflexive particle *sich*, the second "ihr" is a pronoun whose antecedent is "hitz." The assonance of "Ehr' . . . ihr . . . ihr . . . Ehren-ärz" is prominent at the expense of

---

[34] MHG *klenken = schlingen, flechten* (Lexer, *Mittelhochdeutsches Taschenwörterbuch*).
[35] See Peter M. Daly, "Die Metaphorik in den 'Sonetten' der Catharina Regina von Greiffenberg" (Diss. Zürich, 1964), p. 60.

syntactical clarity. The "Ehren-ärz" is both simply gold and, as the last line makes clear, gold in the form of a coin or medal: gold which bears God's picture. The gold is spread about the world; God is made known. Thus the last two lines explain the compound "lob-Gold," into which the steel (= adversity) was transformed in line 11.

These three poems illustrate the basic structural types in the *Geistliche Sonnette*. The structure of the first two poems is very crude indeed: in the absence of any principle of organization and of all management of expenditure, the poems appear simply to have grown that way. Yet both these pieces evince some effort, however ineffectual, to control and form the material within the allotted space. Sonnet 75, the most primitive of the poems, at least has an introduction and a conclusion, albeit feeble, and the flow of examples is not altogether uninterruptedly monotonous. In sonnet 61 the poet recognizes the competence of strophes as component parts of a sonnet. Though she does not enlist these strophes into the service of a larger whole, the poem, she is at pains—all too obviously at pains—to fill them each with a homogeneous discussion. Only in the last example, sonnet 60, do the strophes have genuine bearing upon one another.

Throughout these poems, in each instance to a smaller degree, the poet is troubled ostensibly by a superabundance of unformed material. In fact, her difficulty is an insufficiency of material, an inability to exploit available material. She responds to this difficulty by introducing new material. Her methods are various. In the linear poems she gathers her material row upon row, and it is then her task to enlarge upon a given item and thus to reduce the bulk and sheer weight of this mass, or, as the poem's idea warrants, to exploit the poetic effects inherent in a series of items, to make a virtue of her vice. The poems in discrete blocks exhibit a whole spectrum of methods. The spectrum begins with repetition from strophe to strophe or expansion of one strophe in the next as an orderly means of enlarging the material. It extends across completely undisciplined amassment and culminates in the first programmatic husbanding and arrangement of material apparent in the sonnets. Finally, the integrated sonnets are at their crudest the result of logical schemes. At their finest they represent a full integration of material, idea, and form. The following chapters trace these methods of composition in Greiffenberg's sonnets.

CHAPTER THREE

THE LINEAR POEMS

The basic unit of a linear poem is the line. This is not to say that a linear poem can be reduced entirely to a series of lines. Usually it cannot. It has some kernel, some dense, coherent and irreducible passage or passages which can be recognized as the germ of the sonnet. This germ, however, is meager. To complete the piece, to fill the blank spaces in the mandatory fourteen lines, the poet introduces large quantities of new material in which some portion of the poem's germinal idea inheres. She introduces this material in an orderly fashion—line by line. Each line is a succinct unit of new material, each unit is a single complete thought. Sonnet 17 is paradigmatic:

<pre>
                    17
          GOTTes Vorsehungs-Spiegel.

    DEr Kasten schwebte schon / HErr GOtt / in deinen Sinnen /
als sich der Himmel trübt und sich die Flut anhebt'.
Eh die alt' Erd' ertrank / schon in der neuen lebt
der beeder Welten Held / auf deines Rahts schaubühnen.
    Das Feur war schon gekült / als jene Drey darinnen.
Auch David war gekrönt / weil er in Elend schwebt.
das Weib war schon entzuckt / eh ihr der Drach nachstrebt.
GOtt pflegt die Schnur / eh man in Irrgang komt / zu spinnen.
    Die Schlange war entgifft / eh Paulus sie berührt.
der Freuden-Lehre* Liecht brann schon in GOttes wißen /
ehe man ein Fünklein noch in allen Seelen spürt.
    Vor Unglücks Schickung / ist der Höchst auf Hülff befließen.
drüm folget ihm / wie fremd und seltsam Er euch führt.
sein' Hand hat aus der Höll / geschweig aus Noht / gerißen.

*Evangelium
</pre>

The subject of the poem, which belongs to the group on God's miraculous governance, is divine providence or, more aptly, *Vorsehung*, as in the title. The first quatrain is the germ of the poem. It is a genuine strophe: a full, coherent, and irreducible statement on providence. The statement cites two examples of God's providence; both stem from the Deluge. The first example describes God's provision for Noah and the company aboard the ark, the second God's provision, even then, for human salvation. The second example does not repeat the first. It completes it by endowing God's provision for Noah with new significance. The two examples make a fuller statement than either example alone, and the strophe is an irredicible thought.

Syntactically, too, the strophe is of a piece, even though it is composed of two sentences. The first sentence begins with its principal clause, striking the tonic note of the poem. A subordinate clause follows. The second sentence begins with a subordinate clause and suspends the completion of the sense until line 4, where it coincides with the completion of the strophe and of its sense. The time sequence of the two statements is similarly juxtaposed. The first sentence reverses chronological sequence and mentions the later event first; the second sentence refers first to the earlier event—"alt" precedes "neu." The effect is more than variation for its own sake. The two pairs of lines are counterpoised. They constitute a balanced, rounded strophe, and at the conclusion of line 4 the presentation rests momentarily.

In the first quatrain the poem's impulse is exhausted. To fill the remaining space, the poet introduces new material—a succession of examples which attest to God's foresight.[1] Except for the last example (lines 10-11), each example occupies one line. Each line is a single complete thought, and all the lines repeat a single simple statement: God foresees. From the first quatrain's full and irreducible statement on salvation the poet has extracted one unit of sense and made it the common denominator of a succession of examples. This succession is a list: a series of items which cohere only because they all represent some common property. Aside from this particular coherence, the items are diverse and discrete, and therefore interchangeable. No idea is being developed here; the examples merely repeat one statement at length. Thus they stand in no unalterable intellectual relationship to one another. Materially the examples are related only insofar as they are all biblical and all attest to divine providence. They cite unrelated events of diverse substance, chosen at random from the Old and New Testaments and arranged arbitrarily. No example completes or enlarges the sense of another. Each is succinct and independent of its context. Syntactically the examples are no less self-contained. Each occupies a single line, and each line is a single sentence.

These sentences, moreover, are syntactically uncoordinated. Every sentence begins with its subject, which in all but two cases (lines 8 and 10) is followed by "war" plus a perfect participle, then by the caesura.

---

[1] It might be argued that the poem corresponds to the rhetorical convention which Conrady, *Lateinische Dichtungstradition und deutsche Lyrik des 17. Jahrhunderts* (Bonn, 1962), pp. 128-30, calls "insistierende Nennung." Conrady remarks, p. 129: "Der Wunsch nach insistierendem Nennen ... [ist] eins mit der Lust an rhetorisch-sprachkünstlerischem Gestalten und ständigem Erproben der sprachlichen Mittel und Möglichkeiten." The contrast between the quality of the first quatrain and that of the second would indicate that Greiffenberg was motivated less by an interest in an intricate linguistic gesture than by difficulties with the progress of her piece.

The caesura falls after the third stress of every line except line 8 and lines 10-11, and only in lines 10-11 is the second halfline not a subordinate clause. Thus the caesura falls into breaks between clauses and is doubly intense. The subordinate clauses are introduced by "eh" in lines 7, 8, and 9 and again in line 11. Syntactically the lines are related only insofar as they are virtually uniform. Nowhere does the grammatical structure of one line benefit that of another; nowhere does syntax enlarge meaning. But for the rhyme scheme, lines 5, 6, 7, and 9 are interchangeable.

In the absence of any intellectual, formal, or material development, the lines constitute no real strophes. They remain simply a succession of lines. The effects of this long succession become manifest when one important modification in expression aborts. Line 8 does not cite a biblical example. Instead it uses the present tense to describe God's general and habitual practice in a metaphor of the poet's own making. The remark summarizes the import of lines 5-7. This general summary and a syntactical variation, the complementary infinitive which draws the main clause of the sentence across the whole line, underscore lines 5, 6, and 7 and bring the succession of instances to a halt. The effect is reinforced by the rhyme of "spinnen" in the last line of the quatrain with "darinnen" in the first. With this conclusion of the second quatrain, the first large division of the sonnet presumably is at an end. The pause, however, is only momentary. Line 9 brings another example, again biblical. Its syntax is virtually identical with that in lines 5, 6, and 7. The succession of examples is continuing. The expected culmination in line 8 has proven false, and the succession has lost this possibility of containment. When this fifth example spills over into the sestet, the series becomes tedious and amorphous. The long sentence (lines 10-11) which ends the series can no longer rectify the confusion which followed the false culmination. For this linear poem, as for sonnet 75, (see above, pp. 17-18) a conclusion is difficult. The essential sameness of the succession of examples leaves the poet no choice but to restate the obvious (line 12), followed here by a moral deduction.

The poem is spoiled not only by a false culmination at the obvious point for a true one, but also by the succession of examples itself. The false culmination highlights the great pitfalls of such a succession: intellectual aridness and numbing monotony. When line 9 shows the culmination implied in line 8 to be deceptive, the emptiness and tedium of the sequence become patent. They become patent in the fifth line of the succession. The first four items are still reasonably coherent, the more so if the fourth item might be construed as a true culmination. The succession fails to cohere over a long span.

It fails to cohere for three reasons: it is intellectually static, dwelling on one finished idea; it is formally undifferentiated, repeating this idea by means of identical or equivalent syntactical units; and it is materially boring, citing various instances for the sake of their meaning while it ignores their content. Nothing is said here about the three men in the fiery furnace (Daniel 3, 16-17); David's misery remains unspecified, and the reference is so vague that the biblical passage cannot be identified with certainty; the scene from the Apocalypse (12, 1-16; "entzuckt" = removed from danger) never appears. The reader hardly need even be familiar with these references. He must know only that the examples are all biblical and therefore of incontrovertible veracity, and he must understand their message. They are interesting only insofar as they exhibit these common features. For this reason, examples in a long succession merge behind the common feature they represent, and their specific material disappears. The longer the list, the more insubstantial it becomes.

This proclivity suffices to deprive a list, if not of its usefulness altogether, then certainly of its valid usefulness. It is most obviously useful in inflating poems which are meager at inception. The device is simple and convenient: the poet need only find a common denominator and multiply it at will. She can curtail the series at any point or, conversely, she can extend it as long as she likes. A list lends itself excellently to such employment. Insofar as it is a form at all, it is an open form: its natural tendency is to go on forever. But in going on forever, it vanishes altogether. Certainly it will correct a poem's meagerness, but at great cost: at the price of the poem itself—unless the poet is prudent.

Greiffenberg uses a linear series in two basic situations which greatly influence its performance. Sonnets 75 and 17 are both examples of one situation: the germ of the poem appears in the first quatrain and here the poem's original impulse is exhausted. By means of a long succession of equivalent examples, the poet extends the poem, filling the obligatory number of lines and concluding the series as best she can. This is a free list: the core of the sonnet lies in the first quatrain; the poem has no other visible supports. The list can continue unhindered over the remaining space. In other poems the linear series is not a device to fill space but a method of presentation. The poems in this group are the only satisfactory linear sonnets. They succeed, however, only when they impose logical or syntactical restraints on the series, and, more importantly, when they exploit its material for the qualities which inhere in it. The series is then no longer a list, barren repetition of a single idea, but a quantity of interesting material which form can fructify.

A free list, a series of items which extends a sonnet from its exhausted germ to its fourteenth line, is a list at its most dangerous—a list which, but for the limitation of fourteen lines, can go on forever. Only sonnet 17 on God's providence and sonnet 49, a series of virtuoso variations on the poet's motto "wie Gott wil," contain undiminished lists. Elsewhere Greiffenberg has modified the list by making a number of small changes. All her means of modification are visible in sonnet 108.

108
Auf Christus Wunder-Geburt.

SEht der Wunder Reichs-Versamlung / in der Christgeburt hier an!
der so mit der Erden-Kugel / wie mit einen Apfel / spielt /
wird im Schoß der keuschen Mutter ein geraume Zeit verhüllt.
In das Glas des schwachen Leibes wird der Gottheit Meer gethan.
 Auf daß wir das Leben hätten / wandlet er die Todten-Bahn.
Das uns Uberfluß ergetzet' / er hier lauter Mangel fühlt.
Kurz! diß Wunder-Wunder alles hier, auf unser Heil nur zielt.
Dieses GOttes-Werk kan heissen aller Gnaden offner Plan.
 Die Herzschönste Eden-Blume / blüht in Winters-ungeheur.
In dem grösten Schnee und Kälte / kommt das heissest Liebes-Feur:
daß es unsre kalte Herzen Lieb- und Andacht-hitzig macht.
 Davids-Zweig / hat nun zugleiche / Laub und Blüh' und Frucht gebracht.
Daß der Mensch das Leben hätte / wurd' ein Mensch der Lebens-Fürst.
Seht / wie sehr den Gnaden-Brunnen hat nach unsern Heil gedürst!

    The poem is one of thirteen at the beginning of the collection's second hundred; its subject, broadly, is the birth of Christ. The germ of the poem, the first quatrain, is a coherent strophe. The first line, which reflects the title, is a true topic sentence, presenting an imperial assembly of miracles, which the poem proceeds to enumerate. Not unexpectedly, the poet works with paradoxes, her favored vehicle for expressing the miraculous. Lines 2 and 3 are a single sentence and a single statement incorporating three paradoxes. The principal miracle is that the infinite should be enclosed in the finite. Implied also are the marvels that God should be born and that his mother should be a virgin. The last line of the quatrain underscores the principal miracle with a vivid metaphor. Here again the paradox has multiple implications. "Glas des schwachen Leibes" evokes the fragility and the purity of this virgin body, and makes it into a receptacle; "der Gottheit Meer" implies boundless immensity and power.[2] The two are brought together when the sea is poured into the glass, a process which is both literally attemptable and metaphorically fruitful: it describes not only a miraculous event, but implies also an overwhelming experience. In its archetypally sexual overtones, it suggests the intimacy of the relationship between God and the Virgin and between the Virgin and her child. This terse metaphor wraps up the two preceding lines and brings the quatrain to a full stop.

    Thus it is anticlimactic when the second quatrain resumes the paradoxes and simply plots one quality against another without making any fuller statement. The observations are diverse: only their common quality of paradoxness associates them. A list is beginning, and the poet curtails it instantly. "Kurz!" in line 7 is incongruous. It is too strong a

---

[2] Peter M. Daly, "Die Metaphorik in den 'Sonetten' der Catharina Regina von Greiffenberg" (Diss. Zürich, 1964), pp. 111-12.

word to introduce a summation for two lines. Only lines 5 and 6, however, are still in need of a conclusion; line 4 brought the first quatrain to a full stop. The commentary which follows is similarly incongruous: too weighty and too far-reaching for the two lean lines it is meant to summarize.

For all its emphasis, the commentary in lines 7-8 is ineffectual. In a third quatrain the list sets in again, but this time with a difference. There is some relationship other than paradoxness among the first three lines of this strophe and again between the first line and the fourth line. The first three dwell upon a contrast of heat and cold (merely implicit in "Eden-Blume" = springtime = warmth), and the first and last lines speak of the Christchild as a growing, blossoming plant. Still only rudimentary, the outlines of a coherent strophe emerge from the diverse items of a list.

The last two lines of the poem, its conclusion, are framed still in paradoxes. Line 13 contains a double paradox. "Lebens-Fürst" is a kenning for Christ and the subject of the main clause: "der Lebens-Fürst wurde ein Mensch," itself a paradox with again the paradoxical effect that thereby mortal man attains eternal life. The paradox in line 14 is in the last analysis a play on words: "Gnaden-Brunnen" = God, "hat . . . gedürst" = *hat . . . verlangt*. The two statements are sufficiently broad and gradiose to serve as a conclusion—but not for this particular poem. Line 13 is not objectionable insofar as it is simply another paradox, a double paradox, in a poem whose main vehicle is paradox and whose method is linear accumulation of paradoxes. Line 14, however, extrapolates from line 13 God's great sacrifice in becoming human to save mankind. Certainly this aspect of Christian salvation is present in line 13. Beyond this, however, it is to be found only in lines 5 and 6. These lines were a lapse into irrelevance. The subject of the poem, pronounced in its title, in its germinal first quatrain, and in its third quatrain, is the miraculous birth. The conclusion in lines 13-14 does not apply.

Although the first and the last lines of the poem begin with "seht," the sonnet can hardly be said to have come full circle. The first "seht" points to what is called concretely "der Wunder Reichs-Versamlung," the second to an abstract and invisible process. The formal fluctuations within the piece, moreover, belie any carefully crafted link between its first and last lines.

The poem attempts first to curtail an incipient list with commentary (lines 7-8), then to transform a second linear series by making its items homogeneous (lines 9-12),[3] and finally to finish with an emphatic conclusion. All these measures work to abbreviate the list. The most immediate and obvious are the conclusion and its counterpart, the introduction. These, however, are not particularly valuable in practice. In

---

[3] The attempt aborts because the poet has tried on the one hand to give the items a homogeneous idea (hot-cold), and on the other to introduce homogeneous material ("Blume-Zweig"). The two attempts conflict.

order to reduce a list substantially, they would have to be very long indeed. If a list coheres only over a span of four lines, the introduction would have to occupy the first quatrain and the conclusion the entire sestet. While coherent first quatrains are common among the linear poems and characteristic of a free list, a long and apt conclusion occurs not once. If a conclusion is pertinent, it is perforce brief; if it is lengthy, it inevitably contains extraneous matter. A list is so poor in thought that it never warrants a commodious summation, and the poet is at pains to abbreviate the conclusions of her linear sonnets. A second possibility is commentary. The brief commentary in sonnet 75 was insufficient to break up the list. The commentary in sonnet 108 was equally ineffectual and failed, moreover, to forestall a second list.

There remains one means of controlling a free list: the lines of the poem must be drawn together into some more compelling relationship than succinct repetition of prefabricated thought. Sonnet 83 makes a beginning:

83
Auf die verfolgte doch ununterdruckliche Tugend.

ES ist die gröste Ehr' / unüberwindlich seyn /
und sich auf Herculisch dem Unglück widersetzen.
Am widerstandes Stahl / muß keckheits Schwerd sich wetzen /
damit es schärfer wird / und krieg den Heldenschein.
    Der Lorbeer widersteht dem Feur und Donnerstein.
Die Tugend lässet sich von Boßheit nicht verletzen:
was? die pflegt sie viel mehr zu wundern anzuhetzen.
Die Noht und Unglück / ist der Tugend wunderschrein.
    Was zieret Cyrus Sieg? die widerstandes Waffen.
Es kriegt / durch Kriegen nur / Philippus Sohn die Welt.
Den Zepter / Cesar auch / erst nach dem Streit erhält.
    Nicht faulen Siegern nur / ist Cron und Thron beschaffen.
Drum biet der Noht die Spitz' / und laß dich nichts abwenden:
es schwebt schon über dir / die Kron in GOttes Händen.

A germ in Sonnet 83 is not easily identified. No full and balanced statement degenerates into repetition of its basic idea, line by line. Rather, the examples which repeat the poem's thesis, stated in its first line, are framed in such a fashion that groups of lines cohere syntactically and logically. Strophes crystallize about certain lines. The first line is such a point of crystallization. The three subsequent lines cluster about it. Thus the poem's first potential example, Hercules in line 2, is not cited independently, but in double subordination: as a crucial adverbial modifier within a second, elaborative appositive to "Es ist die gröste Ehr'." The allegory of the whetted sword in lines 3-4 repeats the poem's first statement, but in reverse order. It begins with the confrontation with adversity, counterpart to line 2, and returns to the rewards of overcoming adversity, whereby "Heldenschein" in line 4 corresponds to "die gröste Ehr'" in line 1. The first four lines of the poem are bound up together: line 1 entails the three subsequent lines.

Similarly, the second quatrain clusters about the example of the laurel tree. The emblematic laurel is impervious to lightning, and the emblem was interpreted to signify that virtue withstands evil.[4] Thus the emblematic example in line 5 is followed by its moral application. "Lorbeer" and "Tugend" on the one hand and "Feur und Donnerstein" and "Boßheit" on the other occupy parallel positions. Line 7 sustains the interpretation of the emblem, taking it one step further, as signalled in "was? . . . viel mehr. . . ." In doing so, it ties the emblem to the poem's thesis: the miracles to which evil incites virtue are the counterpart of the heroic sheen on the whetted sword (lines 3-4) and again of the honor in invincibility (line 1). The summary assertion in line 8 underscores line 7 and recapitulates briefly the process by which virtue turns adversity to advantage.

In these first two quatrains examples which might have been items in a list have been elaborated or subordinated, or both, so that they appear in a coherent context. Where an example has been elaborated, it has of course been enlarged and the number of examples required to fill a given space correspondingly reduced. Where an example has been subordinated, it becomes part of a larger fabric surrounding the principal point. No longer are examples listed row upon paratactical row, item by item. Two principal examples, the whetted sword in line 3, which has its proper place within the organization of the first quatrain, and the laurel tree in line 5, which is elaborated to produce the rest of the second quatrain, suffice to fill eight lines.

Thus it is a change of pace when the first tercet mentions three ancient heroes in quick succession. The threefold sequence coheres, the more readily since constantly varied syntax requires that a line be understood for its own content, not as a random example of a larger principle. The series is not simply a catalogue of heroes, but a rapid fire of historical verifications of the poem's thesis. Because the series is brief and graceful, this larger purpose is not lost, and the very rapidity with which the heroes appear serves the larger purpose.

The second tercet, the poem's conclusion, is a happy solution to the problem of a summation for a linear poem. It refrains from restating the content of the foregoing examples. Instead it implies a summation in a negative statement which confirms the valor of the cited heroes by disparaging the indolence of "faule Sieger." The reference to persons not described in the poem is rather a facile transition, but a lesser evil than restating the obvious. It leads smoothly from the heroic examples to the moralizing deduction.

---

[4] Albrecht Schöne, *Emblematik und Drama im Zeitalter des Barock* (München, 1964), p. 87.

In sonnet 83 the poet has overcome the list and its inherent liabilities primarily by elaborating. Whereas in cruder poems she reeled off a long succession of one-line examples, here she has stretched a small number of examples—two—and filled eight lines. Having done so, she can permit herself the luxury of three one-line examples and take advantage of the change in pace. The poem is still essentially linear. The lines appear to draw together, to cluster as it were, about certain points. Ultimately they remain lines. Though they benefit from their context, they could also stand alone, and this propensity becomes more pronounced as the poem progresses. The next step is for the poet to sustain an impulse rather than merely to stretch it: to compose dense, irreducible strophes, simply in series if need be, but strophes which cohere so organically that they cannot be picked apart. That Greiffenberg is capable of such composition is evident in the initial quatrains, the germ strophes, of sonnets 17 and 108. That she can maintain this level of density, or rather that she can achieve it repeatedly in a single poem, sonnet 148 demonstrates.

148
Uber das Wort:
Er ward ein Fluch am Holz.

DEr Segen wird ein Fluch: auf daß der Fluch den Segen
vom Fluch erlangen kan; Gerechtigkeit zur Sünd:
auf daß Rechtfärtigung in ihr die Sünde find.
der Haubt-Gerechte / will die Schuld auf Unschuld legen /
und die selbstschuldigen lossprechen auch dargegen.
Hier lieb' ein Zornes Feur / fürs liebste Herz entzünd.
die Erzempfindlichkeit sich selber überwind /
hasst ihren innern Zweck / der Feinde mit zupflegen.
Es senkt ins Schmerzen-Meer / der Freuden-Ursprung sich.
des Wesens Quell und Ziel / die Selbstheit alles Lustes /
verstürzt sich / uns zu lieb / in Abgrund unsers wustes /
in Sünd- und Schmerzenhöll: so welt-verwunderlich.
Sein' Heiligkeit / wolt nicht des Drachen Rachen fliehen:
daß uns verschlungene sie könt aus solchem ziehen.

The poem belongs to the crucifixion sonnets. It takes as its title Galatians 3, 13: "Christus aber hat uns erlöst von dem Fluch des Gesetzes, da er ward ein Fluch für uns (denn es steht geschrieben: 'Verflucht ist jedermann, der am Holz hängt')." The Jewish law to which Paul alludes is to be found in Leviticus 21, 23: if a man is hanged, "so soll sein Leichnam nicht über Nacht am Holz bleiben, sondern du sollst ihn desselben Tages begraben—denn ein Gehenkter ist verflucht bei Gott." By substituting words and exploiting double meanings, Greiffenberg turns Paul's proof into a triple paradox: "Der Segen wird ein Fluch: auf daß der Fluch den Segen vom Fluch erlangen kan." The first "Segen" is Jesus, who becomes a curse upon the tree. The second halfline assumes this transformation, setting "Fluch" for Jesus. The "Segen" at the end of the line is salvation or eternal life, and "Fluch" in line 2 is original sin or damnation.[5] The statement requires one and one-half lines. In the adjoining one and one-half lines the riddle is rephrased. "Gerechtigkeit" is substituted for "Segen," "Sünd" for "Fluch." "Rechtfärtigung" in line 3 refers to God Father or to divine judgment, the antecedent of "ihr" is "Gerechtigkeit," making the line paradoxical, and the final "Sünde" is the sin of mankind. The choice of words here implies another Pauline passage, Romans 8, 3-4. "Gott . . . sandte seinen Sohn in der Gestalt des sündlichen Fleisches und der Sünde halben und verdammte die Sünde im Fleisch, auf daß die Gerechtigkeit, vom Gesetz erfordert, in uns erfüllt würde." In both passages Paul is at pains to demonstrate that in Christ the old law is superseded; Greiffenberg renders from them the purely Christian concept of redemption through vicarious guilt and atonement, heightening the intricacy of Christ's vicarage for mankind by equating "Fluch" paradoxically with both Christ and original sin and "Sünde" with both Christ and human sin. The complex paradoxes denote also the miraculousness of Christian redemption.

The two statements, which are of a piece because of their common content and common method, are held together also by their abutment at midline, by parallel syntax, and by the elision of the main verb in the second statement. Another elision, an elision in content, makes the three lines cohere. In the first statement Christ assumes the sin of mankind and delivers humanity from damnation. Redemption, however, is a threefold process: Christ assumes the sin, represents mankind before God and atones this sin, and by his vicarage delivers mankind from damnation. The middle step of this process, Christ's vicarage before God, appears only in the second statement. This statement repeats the first step of redemption, the assumption of sin, but omits the third, ultimate deliverance. Only the three lines together describe redemption fully. Since the process is complete within these three lines, the poem tends to rest here. The repose is light. The strophe's countertendency to become quadrilinear curtails it, the more easily since line 4 begins a third rephrasing of the original statement. The first step in the process of redemption was mentioned twice in lines 1-3, the second and third steps only once. Appropriately, the next two lines describe the latter steps once more. These lines are simpler than the foregoing. No longer do double meanings of single words identify Christ with the human situation. The relationship between a word and its referent is unam-

---

[5] Alternatively "Fluch" in the second halfline may be mankind; "Fluch" at the beginning of line 2 may be synonymous with "Fluch" in the first half of line 1. However they are read, the lines say, "Jesus assumed the sin of mankind and thereby mankind gained deliverance," and the two terms of the paradox, "Segen" and "Fluch," carry a total of three meanings:

Segen : *Fluch* = Jesus		*Segen* : *Fluch* = Jesus
Fluch = mankind		*Fluch* = Jesus
Segen = salvation	OR	*Segen* = salvation
Fluch = Jesus		*Fluch* = original sin

biguous. The primary feature of the passage is simple paradoxness, a paradoxness which is not complete until line 4 has been phrased also conversely in line 5. Once line 4 has intruded upon the rest which followed line 3, the first strophe perforce continues over five lines.

Three versions of the process of redemption make up the strophe. None of the versions is complete, so that the double rephrasing is not simply repetition. The first statement, which omits the middle step, is a triple paradox. The second, which supplies this middle step and thus completes the process, contains a double paradox, or a variation upon one basic paradox. Each of these statements requires one and one-half lines. The final statement, which lifts one step of the redemptive process from each of the previous statements and rephrases it, requires two lines; each of these lines contains one paradox, the second being the converse of the first. The dense double meanings in the first statement thin in the second to a single double usage, which is within a hair of being tautological, and to an absence of ambiguity in the third. The poem's original impulse is waning. In line 5 the titular material is exhausted.

But instead of resorting to a series of examples to extend the poem, Greiffenberg retains the technique of the first strophe—paradoxical phrasing and elaborative rephrasing—and applies it to new material, developing another idea. The idea is not entirely new in the poem; it emanates from a shift in emphasis. Both the first strophe and the subsequent strophes ruminate on the crucifixion. The first uses Paul's comment on the crucifixion as a point of departure for reflections on Christian redemption; the second and third strophes reflect on Christ's sufferings at the crucifixion, a topic which was implied in the first five lines of the poem. Common perspective in lines 4-5 and lines 6-8 eases the transition.[6] Both passages describe the deeds of God Father. To this extent the discussion of suffering is introduced obliquely. Only in the third strophe, lines 9-12, does the poet focus directly on Jesus in pain.

The completion of a second strophe is no great problem. Since the first stretched over five lines, this one requires only three. The third strophe, however, the poet sustains over four lines. In both strophes she uses the same method. She begins with a one-line paradox and rephrases it once, using apposition or internal rephrasing (copiously in the third strophe) and parenthetical commentary to enlarge the restatement. The effect, while not brilliant, is much more substantial and graceful than that of a linear series. At last the material is visible, and not only visible, but also exploited. At last the method by which the material is handled is not entirely prescribed. It can now be adapted to the formal needs and the material possibilities of the specific situation.

The conclusion is weak. It applies fully only to the third strophe. It

[6] The construction in line 8.2 is a complementary infinitive to *Zweck* in 8.1. *Pflegen* + gen. pers. = *sich mit freundlicher Sorge annehmen* (Lexer, *Mittelhochdeutsches Handwörterbuch*).

attempts, however, to implicate the whole poem. From all the strophes it extrapolates a common kernel of thought, and in doing so it reduces their respective intellectual intricacies to one pat phrase: Jesus suffered to save us. Only by reducing the strophes to this common denominator can the conclusion bring them together. No single thrust of thought sustains the poem; the strophes are related only insofar as they share this single thought. Their relation to one another is serial.

The liabilities of items in series—intellectual poverty, formal tedium, and material emptiness—can be resolved satisfactorily only when the series is transformed from a device to fill space into a method of conveying information. As the proper method of a poem, the succession's primary potentiality is capaciousness, the positive counterpart of the potential endlessness which made it a useful (and lethal) device for filling empty space. If the available material for a given poem is copious, serial rendition will accommodate it. But this is only a beginning. Sonnet 27, an unembellished catalogue, is a primitive piece.

27
Der GOttes-Wunder Erklingung /
von dem GOtt geleiteten Mose.

ICh der andre Noah / ward' in die Arch von Schilff' erhalten:
kriegt' an stat des Wassers Milch; vor die Hirten Fürsten-zucht;
nahm / vor diesen / jenen Stand / da mich GOtt berufft und sucht' /
schafft' im grün beflammten Busch mich der Schaf des Volks zuwalten.
 Geist-erkeckt / erzehlt ich frey sein geheiß / ob sie schon schalten;
würkte mit dem GOttes-Stab seiner Allmacht Wunder-Frucht;
führt' aus das bedrängte Volk / ganz Siegtragend / nicht in Flucht.
Pharao wurd die Flut ein Dach / uns begunt sie sich zu spalten.
 In der Wüsten / die doch war ein fett Land von GOttes Krafft /
must' uns / die wir Erden sind / selbst der Himmel Brod herregnen.
auff des Höchsten krafft-befehl / gaben Felsen süssen Safft /
 auch der Feur- und Wolken-Thurn schutzt' uns wider all's begegnen.
kurz in einer wunder Sum! mein geschick uñ dise Reiß
ist ein Spiegel: da erscheint GOttes Macht / Güt' Ehr und Preiß.

The subject of the poem is God's miraculous governance, presented here in Moses' experience and told in the first person. The poem merely catalogues Moses' experience, apparently without selection, recounting every major event from his childhood to the deliverance of the Israelites from bondage in Egypt. The material is not only unselected but also unformed. The poem is a series of predominantly simple sentences with compound predicates; one main verb follows another. These predicates in succession usually occupy one line. Enjambements at the end of line 3, where a third verb to the subject "Gott" follows in line 4,[7] between

---

[7] *Walten* + gen. = *bewachen, behüten (Deutsches Wörterbuch)*. The construction is *accusativus cum infinitivo:* "God ... caused ["schafft'"] ... me to watch over the sheep—his people."

lines 9 and 10, the only syntactically dense and fluent passage in the poem, and at the end of line 13 afford the only relief from a monotonous coincidence of the end of a predicate with the end of a line.

The sentences simply retell; they do not cast Moses' experience into any special form. Occasionally a sentence establishes some strained relationship between words and phrases—the most disastrous is "an stat des Wassers Milch" in line 2, where "Wasser" proceeds by association from "Arch von Schilff" in line 1 and produces a painful pun in "kriegen"—but these correspondences are sporadic and without larger significance. The one exception is again lines 9-10, where the paradoxes "Wüste . . . fett land" and, laboriously, "Erden . . . Himmel" imply miraculousness. Otherwise the purport of the lines must be gathered entirely from their content.

The arrangement of the sentences is as unrevealing as their phrasing. The events bear on one another only insofar as they all belong to Moses' biography and appear here in chronological order. Except for the conclusion, where "kurz" signals a summation, the poem divides into strophes only because another sentence opens and the verb moves away from the beginning of the line. The third strophe is not notably distinguished from the two which precede it, and the poem has no true sestet. It is a mass of undifferentiated, unrefined information moving slowly through time. The transgression of the list, especially of the free list, was that its items *meant,* without *being;* their material vanished. The items of this catalogue simply *are,* without *meaning;* their material is vast, weighty, and opaque. At the end of the poem the poet has little choice but to state its meaning outright, injecting a soul into a large and shapeless body.

That such corporeality is not inevitable in a catalogue is patent in sonnet 23:

23
Freud schallender Ausspruch /
des wunderlich geführten Josephs.

GOtt / deß Wunder vorbedacht mich / als ich noch nichts gewesen /
hat zu seiner Allmacht Zeugē / uñ zu seiner Güte ziel /
zu der Glückes-Schickung Ballen / zu der Weißheit Wunderspiel /
kurz / zu seiner Würkung Zweck / ursach-unergründt / erlesen;

zu der Frommen frommen auch / mich verfolget durch die Bösen!
Weil du mit dem Thron umgiengest / ich gleich in die Gruben fiel.
als im Kärker ich gefäßelt / machtest du des Zepters Stiel.
Jene dachten auf den Fall / du auf mein erhöht-genesen.

Ja du gibest deinen Freunden / schlaffend ohne Müh / ihr Glück.
ihres Traums verdeckts Gesicht muß mein Weißheit Spiegel zeigen;
flößest in der andern Siñ mein / in mich ihr / glück hinein /

bringst vom Stock zum Königs-thron / und deß Hungers Kunstgeschick
muß her / daß man hin kan ziehn / dein Volk zur Kunst übung neigen /
daß von ihnen ich / uñ Höchster / du von mir erkandt kanst seyn.

Though the two sonnets are not adjacent,[8] this poem is a companion piece to sonnet 27. Both demonstrate God's miraculous governance by recounting chronologically the biography of a biblical figure, who tells his story in the first person. Even the titles are similar. This poem, however, is vastly superior to the one above. It begins with a long address in a relative clause which encloses a series of items. The relative clause suspends the sense of the series, holding the items together, until the completion of the predicate endows the whole passage with meaning. With the completion of the clause, the purpose of the poem becomes clear: it will speak of God's mysterious and benevolent intervention into Joseph's life. The fifth line is an unfortunate extension of the strophe, which is complete and balanced as a quatrain. The line is particularly awkward because it belongs syntactically to the long relative clause, while it is by content a general description of Joseph's divinely ordained odyssey. As such it introduces the recounting of specific instances which begins in line 6. Because of the conflict between syntax and content, the line belongs properly to neither the first strophe nor the second.

The obvious advantages of the recounting which begins in the second strophe over the recounting in sonnet 27 are brevity and varied syntax. Both lines 6 and 7 are complex sentences beginning with subordinate clauses, but the subjects of the respective subordinate and principal clauses are posed chiastically. The time sequence of the two clauses is similarly counterpoised: line 6 alludes to the historically later event first, line 7 to the earlier. The transposition, seconded by the chiasm of "Thron" and "Zepter," "Grube" and "Kärker," produces equipoise in the sequence of time, and just this stillness is the subject of the lines: all things are simultaneous in the mind of God. Line 8 is a summary of the strophe. "Jene" is a bit vague, having only implied antecedents within the poem: Joseph's brothers, who were responsible for his falling into the pit (Genesis 37, 18-28), and Potiphar's wife, who had him thrown into prison (Genesis 39, 7-20). Thus the line incorporates both events recounted in the strophe.

In the first tercet the recounting continues, but not without differentiation. "Ja" at the beginning of line 9 gives the narration new impetus and appropriately points up what is to be told here: the interpretation of the dreams, the turning point in Joseph's life. The dreams are not recounted singly, but rather brought together as one

---

[8] They appear within the large group on miraculous governance and within a smaller group (nine poems) in which three persons of the Old Testament bear witness to God's providence. The first is Abraham in sonnets 19 and 20. These are followed by two poems on God's "Spiel," the enigmatic game by which he governs the universe, punishing before he rewards (described best in sonnet 66, lines 9-14), then by Joseph's sonnet. Three poems on submission to God follow, then Moses appears. The biblical sonnets appear to be arranged as salients, flanked by and connected by the other poems, which elaborate upon their themes.

event, upon which the poet enlarges. Line 9 is an elaborate double entendre which unravels itself only in line 11. The obvious explanation of "deine Freunde," which belongs to a paraphrase of Psalm 127, 2,[9] is that it is a synecdoche for Joseph. "Glück" would mean *good* fortune, happiness, and the line would describe God's benevolent intervention on Joseph's behalf. "Traum," however, associates line 10 with line 9. The word refers to the dreams of the baker, the butler, and pharaoh (Genesis 40, 5-22; 41, 1-36). "Ihr" at the beginning of line 10, like "jene" in line 8, depends for its antecedent upon common knowledge of the story. "Glück" in line 9 means therefore also destiny, and not only Joseph, but also pharaoh and his servants are implicated in "deine Freunde." The line serves both as a general introduction to the crucial episode in Joseph's biography and as a specific introduction to the precise content of this episode. The same double entendre compounds the sense of line 11, and here it is clear. "Glück," which is elided after "mein," is both Joseph's good fortune and the dreamers' fate: God instilled Joseph's good fortune, his deliverance, in the others' minds in the form of the dreams, and the others' fate in Joseph's mind when he gave Joseph the power to interpret these dreams.

The poem is in full flood and flows without pause from line 11 to the end. Lines 11 and 12 are linked as a compound predicate for an elided "du." Yet line 12 is clearly the beginning of another strophe. Its first halfline résumés Joseph's entire biography in a few syllables ("vom Stock [= Hirtenstock] zum Königs-thron"), wrapping up the poem before the last two and one-half lines bring the crowning event of his lifetime, his brothers' and ultimately his father's trip into Egypt during the famine. Integrated into this crowning event is a larger interpretation of Joseph's biography and thus of God's miraculous governance: in his miracles ("Kunst übung"),[10] his intervention into human affairs, God makes himself known. The interpretation is expressed strictly in terms of its relevance to Joseph's history, but its larger application is clear.

The poem presents only selected events of Joseph's biography—those in which God's intervention on his behalf is especially vivid. These

---

[9] "Es ist umsonst, daß ihr früh aufstehet und hernach lange sitzet und esset euer Brot mit Sorgen; denn seinen Freunden gibt er's schlafend."

[10] "Dein Volk zur Kunst übung neigen" (line 13.2) probably elides *um . . . zu*. The meaning of "Kunst" in the context of God's miraculous governance is explicit in the initial address of sonnet 16:

> DEr du mit Weißheits Safft die Sternen kanst befeuchten /
> daraus das Schicksel wird; zu zeiten ohn ihr Werk
> ein Kunst begebnuß spielst / zu zeigen deine Stärk. . . .

In paraphrase: you can influence—in the original sense of the word—our fate, you can work through the dew falling from the stars (= the natural course of events) or, to show your power, you can work without the help of the stars (= without recourse to nature). An event which lies outside the natural course of things is a miracle, a "Kunst begebnuß."

events are carefully cast. They both *are* within the poem and they *mean* for the sake of the poem's larger purpose; they are both interesting in their own right and intelligible beyond themselves. The events are recounted in series, but in a graduated series. In an initial direct address, an obviously appropriate form for the beginning of a piece, the poem outlines its purpose quite generally. Then it advances to the events themselves, which it arranges chronologically and casts into ascending order, increasing both the urgency of tone and the density of texture in the first tercet. The second tercet résumés the biography in one halfline and goes on to a crowning event, which incorporates a larger meaning for both the biography itself and the poem at large. The sonnet is not a catalogue, but a coordinated and copious whole. This copiousness imbues the whole piece with a sense of abundance—the abundance of God's benevolence and of his benevolent manifestation of himself. From the material form has rendered a threefold idea: abundance, benevolence, and benevolent manifestation.

A linear poem is the product of a series of items. Greiffenberg uses the series to correct meagerness. The corrective device creates more problems than it solves, and the history of the linear poems is an account of the poet's response to these problems. They are resolved satisfactorily only when the linear series itself has been overcome. Though sonnet 83 divides into the quatrains and tercets of an orthodox sonnet, linear strophes enfeeble the poem. Sonnet 148 is the only example of reasonably satisfactory expression in a poem whose initial impulse is exhausted in the first strophe. This strophe is followed not by a linear series but, as it were, by a strophic series: the poem's subsequent lines cohere as strophes whose relationship is serial. The series becomes acceptable only when it is converted from a device to fill space into a method of accommodating large quantities of material. Even then the poem succeeds only if the poet forms the material and if such form makes the material productive of idea. Superabundance of material, however, is not one of Greiffenberg's vices. She continues to be troubled by meagerness, and this study of her sonnets continues to be a study of her means of coping with this meagerness.

CHAPTER FOUR

REPETITION

Well over half of Greiffenberg's sonnets are composed of discrete locks. These poems are central to her method of composition. They range from pieces which, like the linear poems, introduce new material by orderly means, to poems which abandon these devices and, after initial helplessness, begin to conserve and exploit available resources. In these poems appears the first evidence of careful and conscious design. These latter poems are treated in chapter five. The former—those which introduce new material by orderly means—repeat from strophe to strophe.

Repetition was the basic procedure also of the linear poems. The poet repeated a simple thought on a number of examples, line by line. In the poems made up of discrete blocks she repeats not line by line but strophe by strophe. A comparison of sonnet 43 with sonnet 83 (see above, pp. 30-32) shows the fundamental difference.

43
Das beglückende Unglück.

ES dunken uns zwar schwer die Creutz und Trübsal-Zeiten:
Jedoch sie / nach dem Geist / sehr nutzlich seynd und gut:
dieweil / den Palmen gleich / der Christlich Heldenmuht
sich schwinget hoch empor in Widerwärtigkeiten.
 Man pflegt mit grosser Müh die Kräuter zubereiten /
eh man das Oel erlangt / der Kräuter Geist und Blut:
man brennt und läutert sie bey mancher heißer Glut.
So will uns GOttes Raht auch zu der Tugend leiten.
 Es muß das Spiegelglaß sehr wol geschliffen seyn /
sonst ist es nicht gerecht uñ wirffet falschen Schein.
der Mensch / in dem sich GOtt bespiegelt / soll er leuchten /
 so muß durch Creutzes-Stahl er werden zugericht.
Allein in Unglücks-Nacht / siht man das Liecht im Liecht.
uns nutzt das Creutz / als wie dem Feld das Thau-befeuchten.

Both poems state their theses in the first two lines. Sonnet 83 asserts that there is honor in resisting adversity, sonnet 43 that times of adversity and tribulation are advantageous. But whereas in sonnet 83 lines 3-4 double back and demonstrate the thesis by repeating it on an illustrative example, in sonnet 43 these lines move forward and prove the thesis by explaining with the help of the emblematic palm tree, which was thought to grow more strong and straight the more it was burdened,[1] that the thesis is not really self-contradictory. The first quatrain of sonnet 83 covers the same ground twice; the unit of repetition is the line, in this case a pair of lines. In sonnet 43 the thought grows continuously throughout the first quatrain, enlarging from "Tribulation is advantageous" to "Tribulation is advantageous because . . ." Repetition does not begin until the second quatrain.

The second quatrain is the reverse of the first insofar as it begins with an example, a specific instance of "Widerwärtigkeit," the last word in the previous strophe, and concludes with its practical application. The example is detailed and long, thanks to the generality of "mit grosser Müh . . . bereiten" (line 5) which requires another line of elaboration and specification (line 7). When line 8 has associated this example with a process which reflects the poem's thesis, the repetition is complete. Thus the relationship between the first and second quatrains of this poem is analogous to that between the first and second pairs of lines in sonnet 83, and the unit of repetition here is the strophe.

The larger unit of repetition is not achieved without some strain. The example, while not exactly awkward, is nevertheless deliberately long. Its length and detail damage its aptness, for only the two general processes of refinement, the distillation of herbs and divine purification of mankind, correspond. Only insofar as they are both subjected to the same process are "Kräuter" in line 5 and "uns" in line 8 counterparts. The products of the processes of refinement, "Oel . . . Geist und Blut" (line 6) and "Tugend" (line 8), on the other hand, are not comparable, and the comparison suffers from the interpolation of line 6. The tertium comparationis is, of course, that God purifies our souls of sin as the herbalist purifies his plants of their grosser matter, and the purified soul is equivalent to the aromatic essence. The poem, however, does not say so. It substitutes "zu der Tugend leiten." The apodosis of the comparison in line 8, moreover, makes an obvious point, a point which has become abundantly clear in the course of the long description of the refinement of herbs. Line 7, which echoes a number of passages from the Old Testament,[2] is particularly transparent. Since this summation in no way enriches the implications of the comparison, it can only state what the reader already knows.

Nevertheless, this strophe is more concentrated and controlled than the second quatrain in sonnet 83. Here the first line states an emblematic example outright, even though, as line 3 of sonnet 43 shows, one telling word, such as "Palme," in a proper context is sufficient. This proper context sonnet 83 has reserved as a unit unto itself, and the em-

---

[1] Albrecht Schöne, *Emblematik und Drama im Zeitalter des Barock.* (München, 1964), pp. 68-69.
[2] Especially Psalm 66, 10: "Denn, Gott, du hast uns versucht und geläutert, wie das Silber geläutert wird"; but also Proverbs 17,3; Zechariah 13, 9; and Malachi 3, 2-3.

blematic picture is followed by its moral application in line 6. Insofar as an emblematic picture is both res picta and res significans,[3] and insofar as the significance of this particular picture, the laurel withstanding lightning, is (or was) common knowledge, line 6 is tautological, a linear repetition of line 5. This particular emblem, moreover, is not sufficient to reproduce the poem's thesis; the poet is obliged to extend its meaning in line 7. The final line of the quatrain combines the emblem's proper significance with the extension in line 7 and recapitulates. Even though repeating the poem's thesis entails at least three lines of the second quatrain, each of these lines is succinct. In sonnet 43 only line 8 is a separate unit, but the line is indispensable if the distillation of the herbal essence is to be linked explicitly to the poem's thesis, completing the comparison.

In both poems repetition continues beyond the second quatrain. In sonnet 83 it culminates in three one-line examples, whose new urgency marks the beginning of a sestet. In sonnet 43 a second comparison, again with an artisan's handiwork, produces a third quatrain. The transgressions of the comparison in the second strophe are rectified here. The exemplary process is terse, economical, and devoid of preciosity. Its congruence with the process to which it is compared is manifold and full of secondary implications, so that the apodosis greatly enriches the comparison. "Mensch" (line 11) is the counterpart of "Spiegelglaß" (line 9) not only in the context of the rhetorical figure, but in the context also of a whole complex of concepts which Greiffenberg has adopted from the Neoplatonic tradition.[4] The relative clause "in dem sich Gott bespiegelt," which turns man into a mirror, introduces this complex into the poem. In sonnet 10, "Von der hohen Erschaffungs Gnade," and particularly in sonnet 250, the last of the collection, Greiffenberg speaks of creation as an emanation of God. She considers mankind a mirror of God, a conceit prompted probably equally by Neoplatonic thought and by the Judaeo-Christian belief that man was created in the image of God, and she conceives of praise, the essential achievement of a godly life, as a reflection of God's glory back into its source.[5] Man, then, in whom God reflects himself, is a mirror and like a mirror he must be polished—"er muß durch Creutzes-Stahl zugerichtet werden" (line 12). "Creutzes-Stahl" describes neither a real cross nor a real metal. Both terms of the compound mean adversity.[6] In conjunction, "Stahl" endows the adversity described by "Creutz" with a particular harshness, and "Creutz" assures that "Stahl" will be understood correctly in the immediate context, while at the same time it becomes an instrument for preparing a mirror, making "durch Creutzes-Stahl

---

[3] Schöne, *Emblematik*, p. 21.
[4] Franz Koch, *Goethe und Plotin* (Leipzig, 1925), pp. 11-12, describes the Neoplatonic concept of the emanation and continuous reflection of light from an original source.
[5] See sonnet 6, lines 9-14; sonnet 10, line 14; sonnet 25, lines 13-14.
[6] "Creutz" in this usage appears also in the first and the last lines of the poem; "Stahl" in the same usage can be found in sonnet 60, line 12: see above, pp. 21-23.

zurichten" equivalent to "schleifen" in line 9. If man is to reflect God, like a proper mirror he must be polished by "Creutzes-Stahl": if he is to contribute to the greater glory of God, he must be chastened by adversity. The poem's thesis, set forth and proven in its first quatrain, is repeated once in each of the two subsequent quatrains. The two final lines generalize the thesis into maxims. Their function, obviously, is not only to fill space line by line, but also to close the piece sententiously.

In the sonnets which repeat strophically Greiffenberg exhibits greater control of both idea and material than in the linear poems. Instead of extracting from a given statement some fraction of its total thought and repeating it line by line, she is able to avail herself of an entire thought and present it fully once more. In the course of this full presentation she develops and exploits a unit of new material until it fills a strophe. She is no longer obliged to accumulate material line upon line, and the strophes she forms are more than a composite of lines. The poet works with a larger unit.

This larger unit—the strophe—is not without pitfalls. The second quatrain of sonnet 43 shows that Greiffenberg does not always find it easy to fill a full strophe. The deficiency becomes more pronounced when she undertakes to correct the obvious shortcoming of strophic composition—its very strophicness. First she tries to give a poem material continuity. She replaces the diverse materials of sonnet 43 ("Palme . . . Kräuter . . . Spiegelglaß") with related pictures.[7] The criterion that the pictures be materially akin of course restricts her choice, compounds her difficulty in exploiting material, and complicates the correlation between a picture and its referent. Her second attempt, a more promising undertaking, is to make a poem's idea continuous, to open new dimensions of thought even while she repeats. Here the material no longer tyrannizes the piece and dictates its possibilities. Rather, the poet is free to make the pictures serve the poem.

The quality of the poems which repeat by means of pictures depends on both the quality of the pictures themselves and on the quality of the relationship between a picture and its referent. The success of the comparison between man and a mirror in sonnet 43 derives from the extremely economical expression of the example and from the multiplicity of congruences between the example and the process to which it is compared. Similarly, the more modest success of the comparison in the second quatrain can be traced to the circuitous presentation of the distillation of herbal essences and to the obviousness, almost triteness, of the link between this process and divine refinement. The fault is not a major blemish. The poet has left herself free to choose from a broad

---

[7] Because the usual term "images" is burdened, I have chosen "pictures," the English equivalent of *Bilder,* to describe any highly visible material figure—simile, metaphor, or allegory.

range of materials, to select whatever pictures promise to be productive.

When she elects to restrict her material, whether under the duress of her subject matter or in a free attempt to furnish her poem with material continuity, she experiences difficulties. The four *Tränen-Sonette* (sonnets 54-57) are cases in point. The basic thought of all four is that tears mark a turning point in adversity: they bring relief and they bring help. All the sonnets express this thought by representing tears as some other configuration of water, whether by simile or metaphor, and the first three repeat the thought strophe by strophe. Sonnet 54 is in the main a fairly acceptable sustained metaphor of tears as a fountain. Sonnet 56 attempts less successfully to allegorize tears as rainfall. Sonnet 55 is not such an ambitious piece. It contents itself with representing tears on a number of different pictures whose common feature is simply water.

55
[Auf die Thränen.]

GLeich wie der Wolken last in tropfen sich verlieret:
also mein Unglück auch durch Thränen Regenfällt.
als Haubt Plejaden / sie zu feuchten sind bestellt /
der Gottes Güte Land; das hülff-blüh dann gebieret.
   Diß quälend Wellen-Meer an wunsches Port offt führet.
Der Buße Muschel Perl in seinem schoß es hält /
zu dem die Amber sich / das Ruf-Gebet / gesellt.
Offt man darinnen mich / gleich als im Felsen / spüret:
   Sonst treibt die Wasserkunst offt grosses Räderwerck.
Ach daß mein weinen doch auch GOttes Raths-Rad triebe /
daß er dem Sternen gang ein gut geschick vorschriebe!
   Ach Thränen! hättet ihr doch zuverbrennen stärk
die starken Unglücks band. Seyd ihr doch siedend heiß:
kühlt auf das wenigst nur die hitz / weil ihr auch Eyß!

The poem contains five pictures. In the first, lines 1-4, tears are compared to and then transformed into rainfall; in the second, lines 5-8, they become a sea; in the third, lines 9-11, they are equated with the stream which drives a waterwheel; and finally, in lines 12-14, they mutate suddenly from boiling water into ice. The sonnet divides into two four-line and two three-line strophes. These strophes, however, are not unmarred.

The first quatrain gives the poet little trouble. The effortless simile in the first two lines, in which "der Wolken last" und "Unglück" occupy parallel positions, points up the oppressiveness of adversity and thus the relief of weeping. "Regenfallen" at the end of line 2 transforms the tears into rain and enriches the comparison with metaphoric associations. The tears acquire the copiousness and the cathartic effect of a rainstorm. The metaphor is extended into an agricultural allegory, initiated in "Plejaden" (line 3), which, as the constellation which signals the beginning of the planting season, turn the tears into a spring rain. In line 4 excessively precise equivalence burdens the allegory. "Der Gottes Güte Land" is a genitive identification: God's goodness is land which the tears, as spring rainfall, moisten, producing "hülff-blüh," again an identification. The equation of "Güte" with "Land" is necessary because the two are not sensually related and the verb "feuchten" is not sufficiently clearly metaphoric to effect a transformation. For these very reasons overt statement of the equation overtaxes the metaphor. The same punctiliousness of equation appears in "hülff-blüh," and here it is gratuitous. The verbal metaphor "das Land gebiert Hilfe" alone transforms "Hilfe" into the fruit of the land.[8] The net effect of the sustained metaphor is that at some expense it has enlarged the meaning of the first quatrain: tears ameliorate adversity by inducing God to help.

The first line of the second quatrain, which calls the tears a sea, pronounces the basic thought of the first quatrain—that tears mark a turning point in adversity—and thereupon the intellectual impetus of the strophe is spent. The poet fills the remaining lines by plundering her metaphoric sea and equating its contents with spiritual phenomena. The equations are not altogether arbitrary. The traditional association of pearls with tears and sorrow reinforces the genitive identification of pearl with penitence; amber's power to attract (by static electricity) makes it similar to the "Ruf-Gebet," which will call upon God for help. Yet the equations do not really enrich the sense of the passage. The relationship between pearl or amber and the sea, which has induced the poet to use these particular equations, says nothing pertinent about the relationship between penitence or petition and tears. Penitence and petition simply lie at the bottom of a sea, here a sea of tears, and the purpose of their presence there must be read between the lines and reconstructed outside the poem.

The final line of the quatrain is obscure. The antecedent of "darinnen" may be either "Meer" in line 5 or "Amber" in line 7. The latter appears more likely, both by its proximity and because its mineral property makes it comparable to "Fels." Even so "gleich als im Felsen" remains difficult. A connotation of oppressive imprisonment hardly rhymes with "Ruf-Gebet," to which amber is equated. A second possibility is that such enclosure signifies protection and safekeeping, as in sonnet 98, line 10: "in seinem [Christi] Herzen-Felß bistu unüberwindlich." Finally, water from a rock (Numbers 20, 11) is a recurrent motif in the sonnets, commonly designating miraculousness or miraculous productiveness,[9] but such a meaning seems hardly to bear upon "im Felsen" in this context. In fact none of these possible constructions enriches the passage more than another, and it is dubious that line 8 is any more expressly germane to the poem's idea—the salutary

---

[8] Christine Brooke-Rose, *A Grammar of Metaphor*, 2nd. ed. (London, 1965), p. 207.
[9] The motif is to be found in sonnet 31, line 3; sonnet 32, line 5; sonnet 82, line 4; sonnet 125, line 5; sonnet 165, lines 5-6; sonnet 186, line 7.

effect of tears—than the two which precede it.

The first tercet, where tears become a stream to turn a waterwheel, marks a departure from the previous strophes, which is well and good in a superficial interpretation of the proper construct of a sonnet. This departure, however, abruptly turns the assurance that weeping is salutary into an optative whose fulfillment the irreal subjunctive makes remote. Exigencies of rhyme do not explain the new mode. The verbs at the ends of lines 10 and 11 could be changed into primary subjunctive or indicative without great difficulty. In all likelihood the strophe was cast in secondary subjunctive to erase the abruptness of this subjunctive at the end of the second tercet, where the final figure requires it. By introducing this subjunctive already in the first tercet, where it is not conspicuous, given the vagueness of lines 6-8, the poet has circumvented the starkness of a similar reversal of attitude in the last tercet of sonnet 54. The congruence between the waterwheel and its referent, God's counsel, is precarious, resting only on the pun of *Rad* with *Rat*. "Sonst" and "offt" in line 9 betray the poet: she is casting about for new material. The final figure, however, is entirely successful, transforming tears at one stroke from scalding water, evoked by "siedend" in line 13, into ice. The transformation, whose boldness the rhyme of "heiß" and "Eyß" heightens, describes both the feverishness and the desolation of uncontrolled weeping.

When Greiffenberg uses a single picture instead of a number of pictures to repeat a poem's thought, she spares herself such unprofitable analogies as the sea and the waterwheel in sonnet 55. These poems, in which one picture must suffice, are the first evidence of the poet's effort to husband her resources. Sonnets 92 and 93 are both constructed on a single picture. Both have strikingly good first quatrains. In sonnet 93, however, the contrast of light and dark begins to wear thin in the second strophe. In a third quatrain the poet abandons the attempt at a single picture and goes on to new material. Sonnet 92 is based upon the familiar parallel of weather and weeping, which proves more productive:

92
Auf Glückliche Erquick- und Erfreuung.

O Süsser Himmelschluß / auf Regen / Sonnenscheinen /
auf Stürmen / stille Zeit / auf Schnee und wehens Plag /
erblicken nach begier / den blau- und Goldnen Tag!
wer kan / daß Witterung die Sonn verschönt / verneinen?
  wann / wie die Wolken / wir auch unser Angst ausweinen
und schütten / wie der Schnee / mit zittern unsre Klag
die ganz-verwirrt her fankt / und sich nicht halten mag:
da läutert GOtt das Glück / das wir verlohren meynen.
  Auf Gottes Gnaden-Herz / fällt unser klagen-Schnee:
hat einen warmen Grund / der unter sich auf schmelzet;
dann macht die vorsichts-Sonn / daß er von oben geh;

>   die Welt-Erschaffung Hand das Eyse leiß weg welzet /
>   nit sey / bey bößer Zeit und üblem Glück / verzagt!
>   das gibt die gröste Lust / was uns am meinsten plagt.

The first quatrain describes in an exclamation and a series of appositives the divine wisdom in the peace which follows violent weather. Although the appositives all circumscribe one phenomenon, they are carefully varied never to cover the same ground twice. "Regen" contrasts effortlessly with "Sonnenscheinen," which, because it is inflected like an infinitive, assumes the active qualities of a verb, and "stille Zeit" is the natural counterpart of "Stürmen," again an infinitive. The final appositive, which preserves the balancing of pure and verbal nouns, runs fluently through line 3, and its length brings the series to a close. All these lines are immaculate in their simplicity—in the immediacy and naturalness of their expression—and line 3 is of superb acoustical delicacy. The rising, descending, and again rising melody of the vowels, set off by the gentle percussion of plosive consonants at the beginning of every stressed syllable, is clearly audible. The simplicity of syntax and diction and the richness of sound entail no sacrifice of meaning or implication. "Wehen" in line 2 is a latent pun, describing both the movement of the wind and, in conjunction with "Plag," sorrow (*Weh*). The colors in "blau- und Goldner Tag" are symbolic, conjuring up a sun against a clear sky, and a bright landscape. The final line, which summarizes the quatrain in a rhetorical question, expressly names the sun.

The first quatrain has restricted itself rigorously to natural phenomena and deliberately avoided a spiritual parallel. The poet has expended her resources prudently, holding a second quatrain in reserve. In this strophe she entrusts the parallel to simile and solves two problems: the simile makes the spiritual phenomenon's correspondence to the natural phenomena explicit and precise, and yet it does not tax this correspondence by insisting that the particulars of the one phenomenon be transformed exactly into the particulars of the other. This more gentle binding of two realms is especially valuable when the chosen details of juxtaposed processes are incongruent—as is repeatedly the case when two processes are paralleled at length. The sustained metaphors in sonnet 55 forced the poet into dubious equations. Here she can say merely that in weeping and complaint we are similar to clouds and snow; she is not obliged to equate. As in the second line of sonnet 55, metaphoric verbs enrich the comparison. In line 5 "ausweinen" in conjunction with "Wolken" once more makes the weeping copious and cathartic. "Fanken," meaning to flit, to dart, as for example a spark (= *der Fanke*),[10] changes "Klag" (line 6) into snowflakes, which are countless and uncontained. The first three lines of the quatrain are taken up in a temporal clause; line 8 brings the con-

---

[10] *Deutsches Wörterbuch.* See also Horst-Joachim Frank, *Catharina Regina von Greiffenberg: Leben und Welt der barocken Dichterin* (Göttingen, 1967), p. 38.

clusion, the strophe's first reference to the peace and clarity which followed the paroxysms in the first quatrain. There it was the weather which was purified, here human affairs.

At this point sonnet 93 abandons its original picture. In this poem, however, the poet goes on to allegorize in detail the process by which weeping brings help, and in doing so she entangles herself in just the difficulties she evaded by using simile in the second quatrain. She retains the terminology of the comparison and the metaphor of complaint as snow in lines 6-7, but the congruence between the two is lost. No longer does the complaint assume the qualities of snow. Rather, it is forced to behave as only snow behaves: to fall upon a ground and melt there under a sun which are as unconvincing in their equation with God's heart and God's providence as is the snow in this context in its equation with complaint. The equations do not enrich the meanings of their proper terms. The reader discovers in them nothing valuable about the nature of complaint or of God's heart or of his providence. The poet is certainly at liberty to call these things whatever she likes. She must, however, make it worth the reader's while to believe that one thing is another. She has failed to do so here. The allegory merely fills space by extending a picture; it little clarifies the succor in weeping and complaint. The poem's last two lines are, as in sonnet 43, the maxims of a sententious closing.

The poems which repeat on pictures lead from one dilemma to another. If these pictures are unrelated, as in sonnet 43, the poet retains a free choice of materials. She enjoys a full measure of latitude to pick promising pictures on which to repeat the poem's idea, and these pictures give variety to the repetition: they make a poem substantial and its contents visible. Occasionally, within the brief span of one picture, the poet achieves a singularly effective representation, as in the comparison of man to a mirror in sonnet 43, or in the delicate metaphors of faith as oil in a lamp and the poet as a rose in lines 9-14 of sonnet 188. Occasionally, too, the poet is obliged to fill a strophe by improvisation, which she manages well enough in the second quatrain of sonnet 43. At all events, she must content herself with starting anew in every strophe. The disparateness of the pictures breaks a poem conspicuously into hard, fast blocks.

If the pictures are to be materially akin, the poet's choice of materials is sharply restricted. She can no longer choose freely among promising pictures. For the sake of an effective picture she may be obliged to distort the sense of a poem, as in the shift from consolation to despair in sonnets 54 and 55. If she has to settle on an unproductive picture, she has major difficulties in completing a strophe. She must either resign herself to the limitations of her picture and let it lead her away from the point of her poem, as in lines 6-8 of sonnet 55, or, more pronouncedly, in her digression into roses and a snake in the garden in the second quatrain of sonnet 135, or she must force the picture to represent more than it can, as in the willful equations in lines 4 and 10 of sonnet 55. The sonnets built upon a single picture are the first evidence of deliberately managed composition. Instead of pronouncing instantly all she has to say and then casting about for more, Greiffenberg expends her resources carefully. But even when the poet keeps something in reserve, a single picture's productiveness has its limits. Once the picture has given forth all it will give willingly, the poet must either force it, as in the third quatrain of sonnet 92, or she must abandon this picture and try something else, as in sonnet 93.

The problems of repetition on pictures can be resolved satisfactorily in two ways: either the poet makes a virtue of the very disparateness in unrelated pictures and uses this disparateness to transform something dramatically from one thing to another, or with great circumspection and care she chooses a rich and resourceful allegorical material and forms it so judiciously that its references are both clear and convincing. Sonnet 150, on the blood shed on the cross, is an example of the former. In the first quatrain the blood is a golden coin in which salvation and a likeness of Christ are embossed. In the scales of final judgment, the coin outweighs the sins of the world. In the second quatrain the blood becomes commemorative medals ("schaue-Pfenning") dispensed into all the world from a throne of gold and silver. The throne is the wound in Jesus' side, the gold and silver the blood and water from this wound. The medals are very similar to the coins in the first quatrain, but probably not the same. The date which they commemorate is eternity: either the hereafter or the eternity which began with the onset of the Christian era. The third strophe, a four-line stanza at the beginning of the sestet, abruptly turns the poem's imagery wrong-side-out, beginning "Ach weg mit Geld und Welt!" "Geld" here must be dissociated from the coin and the medals in the foregoing strophes; it belongs to a formula for the profane, which concomitantly rejects the elaborate metaphors of the octave. The blood becomes simply a nameless token for which the poet finds a place in the boat that will take her into the other world. In the final couplet the token stored in the ship becomes the sea on which the ship sails, and ultimately, nectar, representative of divine delights in the life eternal. The thought remains the same throughout: the blood Jesus shed on the cross is the sign and source of human salvation. The poem is a tour de force of metaphorical transformation. If the reader consents to play the poet's game, to abandon literal logic and follow her willingly through these transformations, the effect, like the mutation of tears from scalding water into ice in the last two lines of sonnet 55, is intriguing.

Sonnet 222 is a nearly perfect allegory. In this second of twenty-three sonnets on the seasons, the poet takes leave of winter. In casting winter's departure as a burial, she has found allegorical material so suggestive of her subject that she can speak consistently of an interment and yet imply clearly the passing of a season. The allegory can proceed without conspicuous interference. Its progress is so unimpeded for four reasons. The suggestiveness of this particular allegory is no accident. The burial of winter belongs to an ancient European rite of spring.[11] The poet, moreover, has not tried to recount every detail of this interment. Rather, she has selected her material prudently, choosing those points which have some reasonable counterpart in a leavetaking from winter, and she has presented these details carefully, working smaller metaphors into the larger fabric of the general allegory, so that a reference is always clear. Finally, she has not always insisted upon exact correspondence; she is often content with mere suggestion. Thus she has freed herself from the multitudinous difficulties of repetition on consistent pictures: unproductive material, incongruent parallels, excessively precise equivalence, and inordinately explicit statements of equivalence.

The thought of poems which repeat on pictures is essentially static. The pictures are chosen precisely because they represent a certain predetermined idea. If they embody this idea imperfectly, willful equations force them to adopt it, or, failing this, the poem's idea alters abruptly for the sake of the available picture. If a poem does not use pictures as a vehicle of repetition, its thought gains a measure of freedom. No longer controlled by the limitations and possibilities of the pictures, it is constrained only by the principle of repetition, and within this restriction it has latitude for variation and gradation, even for development.

The possibility of variation permits Greiffenberg to eschew the rigid displays of virtuosity to which she resorted when repeating on pictures and to use repetition as the appropriate rendering of a particular sentiment. In sonnet 69 she comforts herself in adversity.

69
Ruhe der unergründlichen verlangen.

NUr ruhe / meine Seel' /in Gottes tieffen wunden.
Versenk' all deine bitt' / in seinem Meer voll Blut:
die kleinheit deiner sach' / in diß Allwesend Gut.
Was das geschöpf versagt / wird in dem Schöpfer funden.
  Sihstu schon keinen trost in dieser Erden-Runden:
wiß / GOtt ist grösser noch / als sie / dein Herz und muht.
Die wunder er allzeit auf über-Irdisch thut.
Ihr wesen wird daraus / wann alles seyn verschwunden.
  Wann Geist-erforschung schon sich weiter nicht erstreckt /
so laß die sinnen in des Glaubens süßheit schlaffen:
dann wird dir Gott daraus ergetzlichkeit erschaffen
  und angenehme Freud / wann er dich wider weckt.

---

[11] Theodor H. Gaster, ed., *The New Golden Bough* (New York, 1959), pp. 251-65.

> Traustu dir höher nicht durch Hoffnung aufzufliegen:
> so bleib' im tieffen grund der { warheit / Allmacht / Güte } GOttes liegen.

The poem never wavers in its soothing reassurance. In every strophe the poet urges herself to trust in God, describing this trust in terms of repose, but always with synonyms. She is not obliged to repeat exactly; she can vary her diction at will and still preserve the import of her original thought. She enjoys freedom of choice not only in vocabulary, but also in the cast of her thought. The bidding that she trust in God has a corollary, first expressed in line 4: "Was das geschöpf versagt / wird in dem Schöpfer funden." The second quatrain is devoted almost entirely to this corollary, making new combinations of its subject and predicate.[12] The third quatrain and the couplet resume the imperatives of repose in lines 1-3 and combine them with again new formulations of line 4. The poem goes nowhere. It circles again and again about the same complex of thought. But this repetition in words and phrases rather than in pictures enables the poet to express herself precisely, while she exploits the effect of recurrent admonition and reassurance. Sonnet 69 is the only example of pure and functional repetition in the collection. Elsewhere Greiffenberg is at pains either to disguise her method or to modify its mechanics. The latter attempt is the more promising.

A repetitive poem can develop genuinely if its basic thought is compound. Such a thought can be divided into facets. If these facets are developed separately, or merely repeated separately, they can join again in new combination at the end of the poem. In Greiffenberg's sonnets the second facet of a compound thought emerges characteristically at the end of the first quatrain. The reminder of God's omnipotence in the fourth line of sonnet 69 is such a second facet. This particular facet, however, does not separate cleanly from the first facet, the admonitions to trust in God in lines 1-3. These admonitions say explicitly that the poet should turn to God, implicitly that her own attempts at something ("deine sach'" in line 3) have been futile, and, implicit in the combination of these two statements, that God can accomplish what she could not. The reminder is formulated to say explicitly that the creature (= the poet) has failed at something which can be found in the creator, implicitly that the poet should turn to God. Thus the import of the reminder, the poet's limited powers and God's omnipotence, is implicit in the admonitions, and the import of the admonitions, the poet's proper recourse at this juncture, implicit in the reminder. In the last analysis

---

[12] The antecedent of "ihr" at the beginning of line 8 is probably "wunder"; the verb is "darauswerden" = to emerge, to become revealed: "The essential nature of the miracles will reveal itself when all creation [= "alles seyn"] has disappeared." In paraphrase, no matter if you find no comfort in this world (line 5); God's miraculous rectification of these things will become manifest in the next (lines 7-8).

the two facets of the poem's basic thought say the same things, but with different emphases. The second quatrain, which elaborates God's omnipotence, continues to imply that the poet should trust in God. When this first facet of thought becomes express again in the third quatrain and the couplet, where the admonitions appear among remarks on the poet's limited and God's unlimited powers, the two facets have not entered into new combination. Their implicit conjunction has merely emerged explicitly. The sonnet's basic thought has behaved as an indivisible unit. For better or worse, its two facets recur throughout the poem.

If a poem is to develop even while repeating, the two facets of its compound thought must be separable, they must be cleanly separated, and the second facet must be elaborated independently of the first, so that when they merge at the end of the poem, the two will form a new combination. In sonnet 134, which belongs to a group of fourteen on the passion, the poet separates the two facets of a compound thought and elaborates the second facet independently.

134
Auf des Traurenden Christi /
herz- und schmerzliches Gebet.

DEr die Erde selbst erschaffen: fällt hie auf sein Angesicht /
auf die Erd. Es betet hier / der aufs höchste anzubeten.
Der uns all' aus Noht erlöst / zaget hie in seinen Nöten.
Ach sein Fußfall / uns im Himmel Ewig das Gesicht aufricht.
    Wie der Fall des ersten Menschen / unsern Unschuld Thurn abbricht:
also fällt der ander' / uns aus dem Schuld-Thurn zu erretten.
Ein Ort / ihn in Abgrund senkt: und das ein' an dieser Ketten
zieht / durch sein Verdienstes-Schwärheit / uns in Gottes Gnaden-Liecht.
    Selbst die Unbeweglichkeit / die dem Felß zersplittert / zittert.
Der die Erden beben macht / bebet selbst vor Furcht und Angst.
Gottes Zornes-Donner ihm alle Aederlein zersplittert:
    daß du deren Heiles-Kräffte / meine Seel / dadurch erlangst;
und der Balsam seines Bluts / vom zerbrochnen Glas / dem Leibe /
sich in dich ergieß' und fließ / Ruch und Ruh in dir verbleibe.

The poem takes as its point of departure the prayer in the garden of Gethsemane[13] and expresses its thought by plotting opposite qualities. It varies the procedure by weighing not only antonyms but also duplicates in antonymous forms or contexts. The first facet of its thought, Jesus' immense and miraculous sacrifice (lines 1-3), is framed in such duplicates. The second facet (line 4) includes the first but alters it by enlarging its meaning: Jesus' suffering and sacrifice are our deliverance.

---

[13] Coincidences with the wording of the Gospels imply that the poem is the precipitate of a devotional: Matthew 26, 39: ". . . fiel nieder auf sein Angesicht und betete"; Mark 14, 35: ". . . fiel auf die Erde und betete."

It is cast in a double antonymy: "Fuß" is opposed to "Gesicht," "fallen" to "aufrichten." The elaborate word play damages the sense, and the line is a bit silly.

The second quatrain elaborates the thought in line 4. Lines 5-6 cast back to Adam, placing redemption in the context of original sin and of all biblical history. Duplicate wording links Jesus to Adam. The duplicates are antonymous and their respective meanings mutually exclusive, so that punning complicates the figure. "Fall" in line 5 is *Sündenfall*, a transgression against God; "fällt" in line 6 describes Jesus' *Fußfall* before God. Since its purpose is "zu erretten," it denotes also his descent into the general suffering which culminated in the crucifixion. In both cases, this "Fall" is in keeping with God's will. In conjunction with the verb "abbrechen," "Unschuld Thurn" in line 5 connotes a protective structure, a fortress, whereas "erretten" in line 6 changes "Schuld-Thurn," mankind's accumulated sin and guilt, into a prison.

In the balance scales of lines 7-8 the poet has found a perfect objectification of the rhetorical figure which has dominated the poem. Like the pairs of duplicate words, the instrument is bisymmetrical, and like the antonymous pairs, whether duplicates or antonyms, its scales are counterpoised. The whole notion of opposite actions probably burdens the representation of redemption more than it facilitates it, but the poet, once she has chosen this manner, has produced an apt picture with which to make its abstractness concrete. More important, the metaphor of the balance scales explains on a natural phenomenon how Jesus' descent, whether into prayer, suffering, or death, has elevated mankind into a state of grace.

Despite its rhyme scheme, the sestet divides both syntactically and by content into two tercets. The first takes up again Jesus' marvelous suffering, expressed still in antonymous word pairs. Line 11 drops the stereotype expression and prepares the way for the metaphor in the second tercet. "Zersplittern" implies that the arteries are of a fragile, brittle material. "Heiles-Kräffte" in line 12, which begins the result clause of the final tercet and turns from Jesus' suffering, the first facet of the poem's basic thought, to the second, mankind's benefit from this sacrifice, is a bold pun. "Heil" means on the one hand Christian salvation, on the other physical healing (as in *Heilmittel*). In its ambiguity lies a second anticipation of the final metaphor, which, much like the process it describes, breaks upon the poem, imbuing it with a singularly beautiful representation of the means by which Jesus' suffering has wrought human salvation. The blood becomes balsam, an aromatic, healing compound, the body—with devastating pathos—a shattered vial from which the balm flows, bringing the soul "Ruch und Ruh": in the form of physical *Heilung*, spiritual *Heil*.[14] The metaphor is

[14] *Ruch* from MHG *ruoch* = *Besorgung, Sorge* (Lexer, *Mittelhochdeutsches Taschenwörterbuch*). *Geruch*, proper to "Balsam," is also present in "Ruch."

systematized elaborately and at length, but at no sacrifice of sense. Quite the contrary. It combines the two facets of the poem's basic thought into a moving, convincing, and vivid explanation of their relatedness, superseding the picture of the scales.

The sonnet is organized like a simple fugue. The first facet of its thought appears alone in lines 1 and 2. In the subject clause of line 3 the second facet, salvation, is heard. It enters fully in line 4. Because the second facet incorporates the first but does not stress it, the two themes are heard together in lines 4-6, but the second facet dominates, and lines 5-6 are given over to its elaboration. In lines 7-8, the picture of the scales, the two facets are brought together—though the second still predominates—and resolved. Because "Abgrund" here, like "fällt" in line 6, is imprecise and in any case no clear designation of the suffering in the first facet, the resolution does not satisfy. In the sestet the first facet is reintroduced and the figure of the fugue begins again—a bit wearisomely since the melody, studied antonymy, is now all too familiar. In line 11 an interesting change sets in. The antonymy disappears; something new begins to emerge and continues to take shape in line 12, which reintroduces the second facet. In line 13 the two facets unite in new combination—the suffering represented by the shattered glass, salvation by the healing ointment—and in line 14 the second facet, in the proper fashion of a fugue, concludes the poem.

Linear accumulation and strophic repetition are standard methods which Greiffenberg uses in executing sonnets. Each method entails a battery of specific problems. The problems are not intrinsic to the composing of a sonnet as such, to the disposition of idea and material within a fourteen-line construct. Rather, they are peculiar to the particular method. In all these poems, then, the poet is preoccupied with resolving special difficulties. She is too much entangled in the possibilities and limitations of her chosen procedure to address herself systematically to the possibilities and limitations of a fourteen-line poem at large.

She attacks the linear poem's tendency to fragment on two fronts: on the one she attempts to abbreviate the list, on the other she tries to make the poem's lines cohere, transforming their contents from items in series to the constituents of a continuous discourse. In both undertakings she meets with only partial success, and she resolves the dilemma only by converting a linear series into a body of raw material which she forms freely. Strophic repetition traps the poet in another complex of difficulties. She can give the strophes material continuity and correct their succinctness, but then the laws which govern pictures hobble a poem. When she does not use pictures as a vehicle of repetition, she is unable to subsume the strophes of a repetitive poem in a genuine course of continuous development unless the two facets of a compound thought make it possible to differentiate strophes legitimately. Because splitting and rearranging the facets of a compound thought is itself a rigorously prescribed procedure, the technique is not widely useful.

Greiffenberg uses these procedures in default of a true means of executing a poem. All fail. The remaining possibility is that she abandon standard methods and compose freely. The worst of these poems are disastrous pieces which come about apparently in the absence of method. When the poet takes cognizance of the limitations and possibilities of a presentation in fourteen lines, however, she can control her greater freedom. She produces sonnets of conscious and deliberate design.

CHAPTER FIVE

AMASSMENT AND ASSIMILATION

Greiffenberg's three standard methods of composition are all means of supplementing a poem's inadequate initial impulse. The disadvantage of these methods is that they each entail a series of special problems, their advantage that they enable the poet to enlarge her poem in an orderly fashion. When Greiffenberg abandons these orderly means, she is still intent upon enlargement. Because she lacks a methodical device, she begins simply to amass material: she introduces it in quantities, irrespective of its relevance to a poem's extant discourse, and she leaves it largely unformed. The characteristic feature of the poems she produces in this fashion is disorder and confusion. The supplementary material subverts the poem's discourse; its relative primitiveness compromises the quality of the poem's expression.

Sonnet 106 "Auf die / der Gottheits-Sonne / aufgehende Freuden-Nacht" is so similar in both idea and material to Gryphius' famous "Uber die Geburt JEsu"[1] that comparison of the two will show both Greiffenberg's difficulty with insufficiency and the effects of her attempt to compensate the insufficiency with amassment.

Gryphius
Uber die Geburt JEsu.

NAcht / mehr denn lichte Nacht! Nacht / lichter als der Tag /
Nacht / heller als die Sonn' / in der das Licht geboren /
Das Gott / der Licht / in Licht wohnhafftig / ihm erkoren:
 O Nacht / die alle Nacht' und Tage trotzen mag!
 O freudenreiche Nacht / in welcher Ach und Klag /
Und Finsternüß / und was sich auff die Welt verschworen
Und Furcht und Höllen-Angst und Schrecken war verlohren.
 Der Himmel bricht! doch fällt numehr kein Donnerschlag.
 Der Zeit und Nächte schuff / ist dise Nacht ankommen!
 Und hat das Recht der Zeit / und Fleisch an sich genommen!

---

[1] My remarks on Gryphius' sonnet draw upon Erich Trunz's interpretation "Fünf Sonette des Andreas Gryphius" in the *Gedächtnisschrift für Robert Petsch* (Hamburg, 1949), pp. 181-86. The text is that of the *Ausgabe letzter Hand, Andreae Gryphii / Freuden / und / Trauer-Spiele / auch / Oden / und / Sonnette* (Breslau, 1663), p. 664; in the von Faber du Faur Collection of the Beinecke Library, Yale University. Reproduced also in *Andreas Gryphius: Dichtungen*, ed. Karl Otto Conrady, Rowohlts Klassiker, 19 (Hamburg, 1968), p. 10.

Und unser Fleisch und Zeit der Ewikeit vermacht.
Der Jammer trübe Nacht / die schwartze Nacht der Sünden
Des Grabes Dunckelheit / muß durch die Nacht verschwinden.
Nacht lichter als der Tag! Nacht mehr denn lichte Nacht!

106
Auf die / der Gottheits-Sonne / aufgehende Freuden-Nacht.

    O Nacht! du kanst dem Tag' ansiegen:
die Himmels-Sonn' in dir anbricht.
Du bringst der Herz- und Heiden Liecht /
von dem wir alle Klarheit kriegen.
    Die Wunder-Kunst wolts also fügen /
das dieses wurd' in dir verricht:
weil in den dunklen Wort man sicht
die grösten Schätz der Weißheit liegen.
    O Ehren-helle Freuden-Nacht!
du hast den rechten Tag gebracht.
Wie kund' es GOtt doch Ewig schaffen /
das Er gewünschter käm' herzu:
in dem wir gleich am bästen schlaffen /
schenkt Er die allersüsste Ruh.

Both poets speak of the night in which Jesus was born; both poets choose to speak of this night in contrastive puns of light and darkness. Gryphius begins with three exclamatory comparisons, each occupying one halfline, which rise steadily, pushing the quatrain toward its peak in the second half of line 2 and in line 3, where the poet discloses the miracle which has made this night bright beyond comprehension. The quatrain ebbs away in a summary encomium to the night: "O Nacht / die alle Nacht' und Tage trotzen mag!" Greiffenberg omits the agitated "Nacht . . . licht" comparisons and begins immediately with a summary statement: "O Nacht! du kanst dem Tag' ansiegen." She goes then directly to the reason, which she states tersely enough: "die Himmels-Sonn' in dir anbricht." The material which Gryphius formed into a swelling quatrain she has used up in two lines. Her third line, "Du bringst der Herz- und Heiden Liecht," consumes Gryphius' entire second quatrain, in which he describes the new era which this bright night has opened. Her fourth, which loses much of its impact to a tautology with the objective genitive "der Herz- und Heiden Liecht," corresponds approximately to Gryphius' second tercet, in which he résumés the deliverance which began in this night. In one quatrain Greiffenberg has covered the ground of Gryphius' full sonnet—and within this quatrain she has said all she has to say.

Her solution is to leap—to a pun on darkness which is altogether unrelated to the complex of light-dark contrasts in the miraculous night: "in den dunklen Wort"—in abstruse writing and speech—one finds the greatest treasures of wisdom. "Schätz" connotes the brilliance of jewels and precious metals, supplying the bright member of the contrast of light and dark.

This analogical interpretation of the reason Jesus was born in the night is also expended in four lines. In lines 9 and 10, a rhymed couplet and a succinct unit between the second quatrain and a concluding four-line strophe, the poet reverts to an address to the night which substantially repeats lines 1 and 2 and might have opened the poem. The reversion is another blind alley. In the final four-line strophe she leaps again, deserting the puns on light and darkness, which are indigenous to her subject and, as Gryphius has demonstrated, fruitful in presenting it, for a pun on "Ruh." The pun is transparent and impoverished. Its two meanings—repose as in sleep and the spiritual solace which is Jesus—are so incompatible that its effect is not unlike that of a poor joke. It is utterly remote from the light that shone in darkness in the first quatrain and the preceding couplet.

Both poems have the same intellectual thrust: an interpretation of the nativity in terms of Christian redemption. Both have the same material: the night of the nativity. And both the same vehicle: paradoxical puns on light and dark. But whereas Gryphius uses the vehicle to exploit his material and develop his idea, Greiffenberg exhausts her topic in the first quatrain. She completes the piece by introducing new material, which supplements the original impulse but wrecks the sonnet.

Greiffenberg has two methods of moderating amassment: she either consolidates the amassed material so that she need not leap constantly from topic to topic, or she reduces the quantity of new material. Accretion is one means of imposing continuity on amassed material. Poems produced in this fashion resemble a run-on sentence: the original thought grows wild. The strophes of the final product are not unrelated, but their relationship is neither good logic nor good form. As in a run-on sentence, the continuity is spurious. Greiffenberg comes closer to rectifying the damage done by amassment when she arranges a poem's original impulse so that the amassed material amounts to no more than an interpolation. Even a single interpolation, however, disfigures a poem by diverting its discourse. The poet resolves her difficulties only when she stops amassing material and begins to exploit a poem's original impulse. Instead of expending the impulse at the beginning of a piece, she arranges for it to occupy an appointed place in her sonnet. The rest of the poem becomes a harmonious setting for this heart of the matter. This is the turning point in Greiffenberg's methods of composition. The poems are consciously and carefully designed, and their design is capacious enough and strong enough to receive and assimilate a quantity of new material. In one final development Greiffenberg enlarges the thought of her poem. Here at last she reaches the root of her problem with insufficiency and takes a decisive step toward pieces of major stature.

The characteristic disjunctiveness of the poems composed by amassing material is thinly disguised in the poems which proceed by accretion. These, too, expend the best part of their inspiration in the opening lines. The poet completes the sonnet not by vaulting from one topic to another, but by permitting the thought to grow at will, governed only by its own momentum—or inertia. Sonnet 37 is one of a small group in which the poet alludes repeatedly to an unadumbrated intention[2] and invokes God's help and support. The poem begins with a splendid rendering of an emblematic picture.

37
Auf meine / auf Gottes Gnad gerichtete /
unabläßliche Hoffnung.

ICh stehe Felsen-fest in meinem hohen hoffen.
Die wellen prellen ab / an meinem steinern Haubt.
So ist dem Meere-Heer / zu stürmen nicht erlaubt.
ihm schadt es nicht / ob schon die unglück Ström es troffen.
   sind manche Glückes Schiff' auch neben bey geloffen:
den rechten / keine Noht / den freuden Anfurt raubt;
das / was sonst keinem ist / ist müglich dem / der glaubt.
die innerst GOttes Krafft steht seiner Würkung offen.
   die ganze Menschlichkeit / (nur Christus ausgeschlossen)
nichts ungeendtes kan / als mit des Glaubens-krafft /
begreiffen; nur durch ihn / wird Göttliches genossen.
   Er saugt aus GOttes Herz der Gnaden süssen Safft:
gefolgt doch' ziehend nicht / weil er ganz überflossen.
der Glaub kom̄t nie zu hoch in sein lieb-Eigenschafft.

The emblem in lines 1-2 appears not as an emblematic proof or illustration but as a transformation of the poet. The transformation begins in the adverb "Felsen-fest," which gives the poet the durability and indestructability, and, by connotation, the altitude and grandeur of a cliff. It is accomplished in "steinern Haubt," which describes not the poet's head, but, since the head is pounded by waves, the apex of a bluff. The poet claims this apex as part of herself (*"mein* steinern Haubt"). She has changed herself into a cliff beset by a stormy sea, into the emblematic representation of her spiritual attitude: stoic constancy.[3] The lines are at once syntactically simple and technically sophisticated. Similar patterns of alliteration and internal rhyme bind the two sentences into a single statement. The alliteration and rhyme rest upon the words which carry the sense of the sentences, and they do not compromise this sense. "Felsen-fest" is idiomatic. "Hohes hoffen" reinforces the connotation of altitude in "Fels," while it describes an exalted

---
[2] See above, p. 15 n. 27.
[3] Albrecht Schöne, *Emblematik und Drama im Zeitalter des Barock* (München, 1964), p. 100.

hope, a hope for something exalted, and, similar to the English idiom "high hopes," an especially lively hope which expresses itself also in a physical attitude: a head held high. The adjacent rhymes in line 2 are more studied and less pregnant than the alliterations and assonances in line 1, but they in no way damage the import of the sentence. These two lines are the only successful passage in the poem. Lines 3 and 4 merely extend the quatrain. Line 3 is not only fatuous, but, as it has been formulated, also untrue. "So" at the beginning of the line was probably intended to be the equivalent of "so that it moves the cliff." As it now stands, however, it refers quite generally to the vehemence of the waves, and that the sea is indeed permitted to storm in this fashion is patent in the very fact that it does so. "Meere-Heer" is a gratuitous rhyme; it enhances neither meaning nor expression. The line confounds the antecedent of "ihm" at the beginning of line 4, which refers of course not to "Heer," but at two removes to "Haubt" in line 2. Line 4 repeats the first halfline of 2 colorlessly and at excessive length.

Sustained accretion begins in the second quatrain. The pithy seascape in the first two lines produces a ship; the emblem becomes a systematic metaphor. Line 6 submits a blank assertion, which line 7 goes on to found, offering the power of faith as an explanation. Line 8 clarifies the statement in line 7 by explaining that the believer has access to divine power. Thus begins the series of explanations which occupies the rest of the poem.

In the sestet the explanations become more and more particular, shredding the power of faith, the belated subject for the poem, into trivial distinctions. The first tercet narrows the sweep on line 8 by explaining that faith is mankind's sole access to the infinite and the divine. The second tercet produces the details to line 11, describing the precise process by which faith partakes of the divine: from God's heart it draws grace in the form of "Safft," which connotes nourishment and comfort. Line 13 cavils at the verb in line 12: grace is not drawn from God's heart; it overflows freely. Line 14 delivers the moral ramification of the distinction in line 13: faith never becomes presumptuous.[4]

The syntax of this passage is as untidy as the argument is picayune. The parenthetical exclusion of Christ from the ranks of mankind (line 9) is a pedantic and unnecessary reservation: among Christians it is generally understood and accepted that Christ belongs essentially not to humankind, but to the Godhead. The remark further obfuscates the antecedent of "ihn" in line 11. The pronoun refers to "Glaube" in line 10, which however appears not as a noun, but strictly speaking as an attribute (and thus, functionally, as an adjective) to "krafft"—hence the obscurity of the antecedent. The whole syntactical infelicity can be

---

[4] The verb "zu hoch kommen" = to become presumptuous. The implication is that "der Gnaden süssen Safft aus Gottes Herz saugen" (line 12) would be impertinent. Hence the correction in line 13. The antecedent of "sein" is "der Glaub": "Because of its characteristic quality—love [*lieb-Eigenschafft*]—faith never becomes presumptuous."

traced to the need for an additional syllable in line 10. The poet inserts "krafft" and changes "Glaube" into a genitive attribute, even though this word is the primary focus of the passage. Once "Glaube" has been established as the antecedent of "ihn" in line 11, "er" at the beginning of line 12 causes no difficulty. "Er" in the second half of line 13, however, refers not to "Glaube," but to "Safft" in line 12. The verb makes this clear, but here, too, the syntax is far from lucid. The poem's thought, which the poet permits to wander once she has expended the original picture of the bluff in the sea, flounders to a conclusion for the first quatrain, recovers in the second, where it gains a new gist, and hacks itself to pieces and into extinction in the sestet. The syntactical imprecision which appeared briefly in the two weak lines at the end of the first quatrain recurs in the sestet and accompanies the thought to its destruction.

The steady dissipation observed in sonnet 37 is ameliorated when the poet uses amassed material only to fill a gap in the poem. Because the execution of the poem does not depend upon amassment, confusion is not inherent in its very composition. The confusion is introduced in a momentary lapse, when the poet inserts into a larger but still insufficient construct unrefined matter which disturbs the poem's intended logic. Sonnet 76 is the first of the cycle on the thwarted trip to a Protestant church.[5]

76
Uber ein zu ruck gegangenes /
doch Christlich- und heiliges Vornemen.

ICh sitze ganz betrübt in diesem grünen Zelt /
muß in der Hoffnung / mich des hoffens ganz verwegen.
Der Himmel ist der Erd geneigt / und mir entgegen /
nimt mir das / wo Er mit verehrt die ganze Welt.
Hat alles seinen Lauff: mein Glück Er nur aufhält /
pflegt dessen Ringel-Pferd viel wehrzäum einzulegen.
Das Schifflein wird verfolgt von tausend Wellen schlägen:
unsägliches Widerspiel den Port-einlauff einstellt.
Doch ist mein Herz ein Felß / an welchem alle Wellen
unwürklich prellen ab. Mein Schluß / ist ohne Schluß.
Werd ich auch schon genetzt von meiner Thränen quellen:
mein Felsenhaffter Sinn jedoch nicht weichen muß /
will / läst mich Unglück nicht in wunsches-Hafen lauffen /
ehe ichs verlaß / mein Liecht umarmend eh ersauffen!

The poem opens with a description of the poet's physical surroundings from which she extrapolates a contrary description of her spiritual state. She sits *sadly* in green surroundings, perhaps in a leafy shelter in the woods, perhaps on the open countryside. Green is the color of hope, and the poet uses parallelism to make it perfectly clear that the color is

[5] See above, p. 16.

also symbolic: "Ich sitze . . . *in* diesem grünen Zelt . . . *in* der Hoffnung." Nature's symbol, however, is deceptive. Here under the sign of hope the poet must renounce all hope.[6] Lines 3-4 present a similar contradiction between the poet's natural surroundings and her personal situation. "Der Himmel ist der Erd geneigt" describes both the incline of heaven arching over the earth and, figuratively, heaven's favorable disposition toward earth. From the poet, on the other hand, heaven withdraws the favor it bestows upon all the world. The poet, then, is out of harmony with nature. She has suffered an unreasonable and inexplicable reversal of her fortunes. At this point Greiffenberg is content to let the adversity remain unexplicated. She reserves her construal of the misfortune as a harbinger of greater blessing for sonnets 79 and 80.

In the second quatrain the poet pivots. In line 5 she accepts her misfortune as a temporary obstruction in the fulfillment of her happiness. In line 6 she repeats this sentiment on a picture of a jousting horse, and in lines 7-8 she digresses into an allegory of a sea voyage. Here she loses the thrust of the thought in lines 5-6 and simply describes her adversity. The discourse regresses to its state of development in the first quatrain. It regresses even further, for now the interesting discrepancy between nature and the poet is missing. From the traditional allegory, which becomes a pointless circumlocution in the absence of any secondary implications, the reader learns nothing he did not know before. Intellectually, then, the strophe is largely void. Only line 5 brings new information to advance the discourse. Line 6 repeats line 5 without enriching it. Lines 7-8 retreat into clichés and unenlightening generalities.

Line 9 moves forward again. It pivots sharply from lines 7-8, pronouncing the poet's defiance of her misfortunes. In lines 7-8, however, the poem's discourse retreated to a point behind lines 5-6, and lines 5-6 have already pivoted, so that the sharp about-face indicated by "doch" at the beginning of line 9 becomes a non sequitur. The imagery also clashes. In the allegory of the sea voyage, the poet is a ship, the voyage is his life, and the port is the goal of his voyage (= his life), usually the completion of his life and his entry into the beyond. In line 9, however, the poet's heart has become a bluff, which can hardly be reconciled with the poet as a ship. The two seascapes are incompatible; the one excludes the other.

The discourse in lines 9-14 is continuous, and the imagery is managed so that it never dominates this discourse. The opening sentence describes an attitude which the poet maintains throughout the sestet. The metaphor of her heart as a bluff that withstands an onslaught of waves deliberately evokes the emblem of stoic constancy. In its capacity as a metaphor it gives the heart, the seat of the sentiments, a bluff's proud bearing and impregnability. The second halfline of 10 is an in-

---

[6] *sich verwegen* + gen. = *etwas verloren geben: Deutsches Wörterbuch.*

nocuous pun. It bears out and reinforces the sentiment of the previous sentence and, more important, curtails the picture before it can ossify into an allegorical landscape. Lines 11-12 suggest the picture in lines 9-10.1 without reconstituting it. The poet's tears are "quellen"; the poet herself, who is moistened by these tears, becomes an indeterminate geographical formation. Her "Sinn," the equivalent of "Herz" in line 9, is no longer a "Felß," but merely "Felsenhafft." It assumes the qualities of a bluff, exaltedness and unyieldingness, without undergoing transformation. "Weichen" in line 12 is a pun whose one sense is consistent with the metaphor, while the other gives the metaphor meaning beyond itself: a geographical formation can be softened (*erweichen*) by water; the poet's "Felsenhaffter Sinn," however, must not relent (*weichen*), for all the unhappiness (= "Thränen") resistance may cost her. The picture in lines 11-12 draws upon the emblem at the beginning of the sestet without sustaining the original metaphor. The geographical formation here never emerges as a clear landscape.

Thus the landscape which rises out of the final couplet encounters no opposition, while it takes material continuity from "Felsenhafft," the surviving remnant of the first seascape. "Wunsches-Hafen" in line 13 alludes to the traditional allegory of the sea voyage without reviving it. Since the allegory was the common property of the age, the very brief allusion suffices to evoke all its implications. The poet assumes this common knowledge and takes advantage of it. She forgoes the allegory itself and exploits its landscape, which she need not even describe, to found a metaphor of her own. In a troubled sea, Jesus, the light of the world, becomes a beacon, a buoy, which the poet embraces, even to her own destruction. In a series of independent metaphors derived from one general realm, the poet has produced a continuous and logical exposition of her spiritual state.

The clash between the sestet and the second quatrain can be explained if this quatrain is assumed to be secondary, if not to the poem's actual composition, then at least to its conception. If the second quatrain is omitted, the third follows from the first. The allegory of the sea voyage is not a necessary transition to the bluff in the sea, for the latter, particularly in its capacity as an emblem, is a self-explanatory figure. The second quatrain, moreover, is the weakest section of the poem. Its pertinent content is minimal, its expression tepid, its metaphors barren. The poem then, as it was conceived, would consist of a description of the poet's personal situation and an exposition of the attitude she adopts toward her misfortune. This two-step process did not suffice to fill fourteen lines. The poet amassed a second quatrain from available bits and pieces of reasoning and imagery, and interpolated it into her plan. The interpolation destroyed the logic of her piece.

This logical plan for the execution of the poem is unprecedented. In the linear poems and in the repetitive poems made up of discrete blocks, the standard methods of composition substituted for an intellectual design. The more primitive of the amassed poems owe their very primitiveness, their disorder, to the absence of both a methodical device and an intellectual design. In sonnet 76 a basic order is discernible, for all its disfigurement in the final product. It has been disfigured because the plan for the poem made no allowance for the material which ultimately was interpolated. The poet split the basic idea of the poem, but she did not prepare herself to fill the gap between the first quatrain and the sestet coherently. She made no arrangements for the new material to occupy an articulate position within her larger design.

When instead of amassing Greiffenberg takes advantage of the initial impulse of her poems, she achieves continuous discourse even in the absence of a methodical device. For this impulse she composes a coherent setting. The sonnets become consistent constructs into which the poet assimilates material. Intensifying the tone of the delivery is the more primitive and the more confining of Greiffenberg's procedures for the assimilative sonnets. When she freely enlarges the setting for a poem's principal idea, her composition gains new latitude.

Sonnet 164, composed by intensification, is the third poem on the seven wonders attendant upon Jesus' death.

164
Das Erd-beben.

EY was! nit beben nur / ich solte ganz zerspringen;
den Mittel-punct mein Herz mitleidigst schütten aus.
Erschütt- und Zittern soll ich vor den starken Braus
der Seuffzer Winde / die sich aus den Hölen schwingen.
Der Stürme Schwerd mir soll durch Herz und Nieren dringen.
Die Berg verbergen auch der Wunder-Schmerzen Strauß /
und in die innerst Klufft das höchste Adler-Hauß:
dieweil der Tod jetzt kam / das Leben umzubringen.
Das Wort / durch daß ich ward / der Athem / der mich schuff /
mein Seel' und Quelle / stirbt: und ich solt nicht erschrecken /
und zeigen Schmerz und Leid? durch Beben / ich ausruff /
daß GOtt liebt /leidt und stirbt / auf mir / in allen Ecken.
Mensch / der du auch bist Erd' / erbeb auch und erschrick!
denk / was das Leben tödt / sind deine Sünden-Tück.

As in the other sonnets on the wonders, the party to the miraculous phenomenon speaks in the first person. The earth takes up a challenge here, and this setting for her discourse justifies the growing urgency of her delivery. In line 1 she brushes aside the title, and the tone immediately begins to rise. It will reach great heights at its culmination. The earth's reply to her hypothetical interlocutor is that she should respond with a proper cataclysm to a catastrophe which is not yet specified but is generally understood within the group of sonnets. Line 1 contains the substance of the earth's retort and a sample of its manner. The poet does not withhold. Her method is to magnify and reinforce what is already known. The subsequent lines of the quatrain deliver the details to line 1. Line 2 is pregnant beyond appearances. "Mein Herz . . . ausschütten" is innocuous enough, but "den Mittel-punct . . . ausschütten" is as much as to say that the earth should turn herself wrong side out. "Mitleidigst" also contains more than a purely subjective sentiment. Both these expressions are planted here. They become fruitful in the second quatrain. Lines 3-4 describe the earth's proper reaction specifically, and their concrete details begin an account of a convulsion in nature. The preponderant sibilants in line 3 are unmistakable. They recur in such density throughout the greater part of the poem that the reader's ear, once attuned to their sound, hears them also in the lines in which they are scant. Their harsh hiss evokes both the force of the cataclysm and the intensity of the emotions which prompt the earth to speak.

The second quatrain begins with a drastic metaphoric description of the cataclysm, punctuated by fourfold sibilance. The metaphor recalls Simeon's prophecy to Mary at the temple—"und es wird ein Schwert durch deine Seele dringen" (Luke 2, 35)—and its traditional representation in the Stabat mater and in paintings of the Mater dolorosa. By association, the earth becomes Jesus' bereaved mother. In lines 9-10.1 she becomes his daughter. The discourse returns promptly to the plainspoken details of the cataclysm and depicts the reactions of the earth's component parts, implying the great dimensions of the response to the still unnamed catastrophe. "Der Wunder-Schmerzen" in line 6 is a genitive plural which modifies "Strauß," the direct object of the clause. The line echoes Jesus' apocalyptic prediction to the women who followed him to Calvary: "Dann werden sie anfangen, zu sagen zu den Bergen: Fallet über uns! und zu den Hügeln: Decket uns!" (Luke 23, 30). The line also begins a figure which emerges in line 7. Here the verb is understood from lines 5 and 6: "die Berge sollen das höchste Adlerhaus in die innerste Kluft verbergen." The world upside down,[7] nature out of joint: the implications of "den Mittel-punct . . . ausschütten" in line 2 become explicit. Line 8 is the poem's first culmination. The sibilants disappear, for the line is pure meaning, pure explanation. It names the catastrophe which has brought forth this cataclysm and explains the relationship between the catastrophe and the cataclysm. "Das Leben," a metonym for Jesus, but also that which is quintessentially life, is dead. In the catastrophe, too, nature is out of joint. In sympathetic response—which discloses the deeper meaning of "mitleidigst" in line 2—the earth turns herself upside down.

The third strophe, a quatrain, belongs to the sestet. With new im-

---

[7] See Ernst Robert Curtius, *Europäische Literatur und lateinisches Mittelalter* (Bern, 1948), pp. 102-06.

petus, with a renewed and intensified response—an incredulous question—to a hypothetical interlocutor, it begins a cadenza. Like the first line of the second quatrain, which elaborated "Winde" into "Stürme," line 9 picks up and builds upon the last line of the previous strophe. The catastrophe to which the earth responds has now been named, and she can elaborate it with details, rising through the fivefold sibilance of lines 10-11.1 to a final culmination in line 12.1—the precise and explicit description of the catastrophe, made sharply articulate in monosyllabic words: "daß Gott liebt / leidt und stirbt." The concluding couplet is disastrously anticlimactic. Its only justification is that Greiffenberg adheres here to the practice she follows in five of the group of seven sonnets: the poems conclude with an admonition to mankind. The poem has assimilated an immense amount of material—the specific details of the cataclysm and an elaborate circumscription and description of the catastrophe. All these bits of information have been subsumed into the continuum of a single protest, and the two events which are the subject of the poem have been faultlessly meshed.

The sonnets which introduce new material into an intensifying delivery mark the appearance of programmatic frugality of poetic presentation. Heretofore the poet's practice has been to come forth promptly with the heart of her matter, to expend the better part of a poem's impetus at the beginning of the piece and then to supplement this impetus. Here the heart of the matter still appears at the beginning of the piece, but the full force of the delivery emerges only in the course of the presentation. The apex of the poem is thus achieved at a designated place within a controlled design. But this apex can be reached only by means of continuous magnification.

An enlarged setting for a poem's idea permits the poet to approach the pinnacle of her piece by other routes. Form in her poems is on its way to becoming freely determined. Sonnet 195 is the first of the poems on the Trinity which conclude the second hundred.

195
Uber die Allerheiligste Göttliche Dreyeinigkeit.

DRey-Einig-Einig-Drey! auf nie begriffne Weise /
ist Gott das höchste Gut / des Wesens Wesenheit /
des Ursprungs Ur-Ursprung und Ewig vor der Zeit /
des Worts und Athems Safft / und alles Lebens Speise!
  in jedlicher Person ich Christ-verständig preise
die GOttes Fülle / ja die Haubt-Vollständigkeit:
und doch derselben Seyn zertheilet nicht ausbreit.
bey meinem Seelen-Heil / geh' ich hierinnen leise?
    die innerst Einigkeit in diesem Drey besteht /
welch' unvermängbar aus dem Einzeln Wesen geht:
zwo Ewig Einige doch unterschiedne Sachen!

>GOtt-Vatter / Sohn und Geist / du Einig wahrer GOtt!
>verzeih mirs / daß ich dich verklär / die ich nur Koht.
>dein Klarheit will sich auch im duncklen sichtbar machen.

The relevant part of the poem divides into three sections. The first quatrain invokes the Trinity, the most mysterious and incomprehensible of Christian dogmas. The second quatrain raises a challenge to this mystery. The first tercet affirms the mystery and resolves the challenge. Except for the address in line 12, the second tercet is irrelevant. The exclamation in the first halfline, which names the fundamental quality of the Trinity and rephrases it with inversion, recreates the central mystery of the dogma: God is three and yet one, one and yet three—as difficult of comprehension as the full circle of contradiction which describes him. The line goes on to mention explicitly the incomprehensibility of this mystery in an adverbial phrase which begins a description of God as both one and three. In line 2 God is one. The word "Gott" does not distinguish among the three persons, nor do the predicate nouns which call him the summum bonum, the essence of being. The latter term is a point of departure for three equations in lines 3-4. All three speak of God as the original source, so that within the Neoplatonic tradition they describe one being. In a more strictly biblical context, however, and in the context of other sonnets, the equations distinguish among the three persons. The most obvious is "alles Lebens Speise" for the son, who is called "das Brod" in sonnet 113 on the nativity and is associated with bread many times in the communion sonnets. "Des Worts und Athems Safft" refers to the spirit, which hovered over the waters before the beginning of time, which, as the word, was in the beginning, which God breathed into Adam, and which came to the gathering at Pentecost in the form of a rushing wind. "Des Ursprungs Ur-Ursprung" is so Neoplatonic in concept and expression that it can hardly be reconciled with Christian orthodoxy. Only the father remains. In sonnet 196, line 2 and line 13, also on the Trinity, Greiffenberg speaks of him first specifically and then exclusively as the creator. This is the closest connection which can be drawn between the expression in line 3.1 and the first person of the Trinity. The three persons are still equated by the verb *to be* and by their common property of Neoplatonic originality with the one being God.

In the second quatrain, the poet describes what she has done in the first. In keeping with Christian thought ("Christ-verständig") she has praised God's completeness in each person, and yet she has not divided this completeness into three persons. In line 8 she raises a challenge to her course of action in the form of a question: is it timidity to have adhered to the letter of the doctrine which proclaims that God is neither three nor one, but both three and one? The oath with which she formulates the question is no idle expletive: her salvation depends upon the validity of the doctrine which she espouses.

The first tercet reaches the heart of the matter and affirms the Trinity, not in terms of Christian dogma or doctrine, but in terms of the poet's own convictions. In lines 9-10 she proclaims the truth of the Trinity on her own responsibility, reversing, rephrasing, and expanding the circular paradox of the first halfline. Line 9 enlarges upon "Einig-Drey" and reinforces the idea of oneness by making "Drey" singular: "in diese*m* Drey." Line 10 echoes "Drey-Einig": "unvermängbar" implies the plurality of "Drey," to which it is related through the relative pronoun "welch'," while "Wesen" is singular and describes the one being which is God. Line 11 extracts from the mystery of the Trinity its fundamental paradox: oneness and threeness, unity and plurality, are two different things which as a religious truth are eternally one.

The formula of address in line 12 expresses again the mysterious concept. For the first time the three persons of the Godhead are named, but no sooner have they been distinguished than they are recombined. "Du Einig wahrer Gott" describes both the one true God ("Einig" = *einzig*) and the true God who is, though three persons, one. Here, as in sonnet 164, the twelfth line would be a fitting conclusion to the poem. The naming of the persons and then of the one God would serve not as an address, but as a final one-line affirmation of the Trinity. This conclusion falls short of the requisite fourteen lines, and the poet appends a new problem, which she promptly solves. But for this one last lapse, the sonnet divides tidily into an introduction which furnishes a basis for a dispute, the point of dispute itself, and the resolution of the dispute—the affirmation of the Trinity on the poet's own terms, which is both the core of the poem and the heart of its matter.

Intensification and an enlarged setting are dilatory tactics to save the main thrust of a poem's idea for the proper moment. The intellectual content of the poems composed by these procedures is small, and the poet economizes with it gracefully, working it into a harmonious larger setting. This larger setting is a conscious design. With the possibility of an intelligent design the poet enjoys a large measure of freedom in the execution of her poems. She does not confine herself to the rigors of a specified method of execution, and the vagaries of the method do not tyrannize her. She has emerged from the morass of an absence of method. And yet she is not altogether free to arrange her poems entirely according to her needs and desires. By reserving the core of a poem's intellectual substance to a chosen place, she constrains herself to work toward a designated high point. To this extent the movement of a poem's thought is prescribed, and it is this preordination of the exposition which distinguishes these poems, for all their fine formal qualities, from the fully integrated sonnets. Their thought is essentially stable. Somewhere in the course of the poem it simply emerges in full, and the sonnet is arranged around this moment of appearance. If a sonnet is to be fully integrated, its form must be independent of such restraint. Idea, material, and form must accommodate one another mutually. A poem's thought, in a word, must grow.

In the last group of the poems which are neither composed by a standard method nor yet truly integrated, Greiffenberg ventures into enlarging the intellectual format of her sonnets. The step damages her technical finesse. She had almost perfect control of her more modest attempts at intensification and enlarged setting. In this more ambitious undertaking she falters momentarily. Sonnet 96 is one of the last of the large group on adversity. The poet expresses her joy upon emerging from tribulation.

96
Uber ein unverhofft beschertes Hülff-Glück.

BIllich / weil dein Güt' im Herzen / ist dein Lob in meinem Mund /
O du Glück und Herzen HErr! du kanst Freud und Wundermachen /
auch in einem Augenblick. Hätt ich aller Engel Sprachen:
deines Lobes minsten theil / ich doch nicht aussprechen kund.
Herzens-Angst in Herzen Freude wandelstu / in einer Stund.
Deiner vorsicht Weißheit-Aug / muß vor unsre Wolfart wachen /
und so wunder Heiliglich ordnē unsre Lebens-sachē /
das von deiner Gnad wolthaten / ganz erschallt das grosse Rund.
Ach mein König / Priester / Hirt! wollest Herrschen / Opfern / weiden
über Seel / die Sünd / im wort / das ich lerne frefel meiden.
Was soll ich / mein Hort / dir geben? mein Herz? ists doch deine Gab /
die / zu tausend andern / du mir in diesem Leben geben?
was denn? ist doch dein schon alles / was ich kan / weiß / bin und hab.
Heyland! gieb / zum überfluß / dir zu Lob und Ehr zu leben!

The poem divides into three sections. In the first the poet reacts to her new-found happiness with a desire to praise God. In the second, the middle of the poem, she praises God, and in praising him she describes what he has done for her. In the third she raises her praise to a desire to present God with a gift. These three sections break the sonnet unorthodoxly. The first occupies the first quatrain, though not entirely consistently. The second takes up the second quatrain and runs on into two adjoining lines which are rhymed as a couplet. The last section, like the first, is four lines long.

The first line comes immediately to the point: the poet intends to praise God. She is not playing for time here either by speaking vaguely and withholding information or by keeping herself on the periphery of some central thought. The parallelism of "Güt' im Herzen" and "Lob [im] . . . Mund," together with the causal "weil," makes the relationship between the poet and God direct and reciprocal beyond the prose sense of the line. The formula of address to God in line 2 reveals in what capacity he is being approached here. "Herzen Herr" is not only a word of endearment but also a compound, to which "Glück," despite the absence of a hyphen, is also a term: God is the master of the poet's fortunes and the ruler of her heart. The second halfline of 2 and the first of 3 are a lapse in continuity. The poet plunges straight into praise, provoked probably by the import of the formula of address. She has described God as the master of fate and goes on to explain how he can intervene into a course of events. But she is not yet through with her preliminary expression of desire to praise, to which she reverts in the second halfline of 3. By mentioning the infinitely small ("nicht den minsten theil"), the sentence which begins here opens the unachievable dimensions of the infinitely large. It has a ring of finality. Obviously it closes the strophe; it almost closes the poem.

The second strophe goes from the expression of a desire to praise into praise itself. Line 5 reproduces almost exactly the import of lines 2.2-3.1, showing these to have been premature. "Herz" here is formally unrelated to "Herz" in line 2, which in turn has no bearing on the same word in line 1. In line 5 it magnifies the qualities "Angst" and "Freud" by making them intensely subjective. Line 6 begins a long and fluent sentence whose sweep embraces God's full competence as "Glück und Herzen Herr" ("vorsicht" = *Vorsehung*) and comes round again in line 8 to the praise motif of the first strophe. "Erschallen" in line 8 gains particular aptness from "das grosse Rund," which describes not only the macrocosm, but also a geometric structure in which sound is especially given to reverberation.

Lines 9-10, a couplet, move from a description of God's rule over fate to an exhortation that God take the poet into his keeping. The transition is somewhat abrupt, but these lines are logically related to the four above and extend the second quatrain into a long midsection of the poem. The versus rapportati with double meshing of three members condense a detailed petition into a very brief passage, leaving room for the poem's thought to enter another stage before the end of the sonnet. God should take charge of the poet's soul, purge her of her sin, and instruct her, keeping her on the paths of righteousness.

The final strophe surpasses the impulse to praise, which has dominated the poem to this point, with a desire to give God something. The poet turns this desire into a dilemma: all that she can offer belongs already to God. The dilemma is neither new nor unusual in Christian thought. The poet refreshes the old problem by producing a surprising resolution: since she can give nothing, God should grant, in addition to all he has already given, that she can live to praise and honor him. The solution ties the final strophe again to the rest of the poem, which speaks at length of God's generosity: even the power to praise is a gift of God.

The poem is hardly an example of great technical refinement. Its unorthodox strophes ignore the best possibilities of the sonnet as a form. An awkward anticipation of the content of the second strophe interrupts the discourse of the first. A crude joint at line 9 changes the second strophe into a midsection of six lines. The word "Herz" appears five times; only the two occurrences in line 5 are related. And yet the poem is of considerable intellectual substance. Each strophe is a solid discourse on a particular topic, and these topics are all closely related within the larger field of the poet's reaction to a new happiness, so that the strophes follow logically. In the first the poet expresses her desire to praise. In the second she praises, and the substance of her praise is germane. In the third she surpasses her praise with an impulse toward personal generosity, and she resolves this impulse by returning to God's generosity, which has prompted and sustained the poem. The poem's intellectual substance grows. In each strophe it puts out new shoots, which are controlled and disciplined never to grow wild. What the piece lacks is a fine technical integration of these strophes, so that they follow not only logically, but also formally, building one irreducible construct which is a sonnet.

When Greiffenberg eschews her standard methods of composition, she loses control of her poems. She overcompensates for the loss of an automatic means of extending a poem by grasping after new material, which she introduces hastily. The new material enters either in a largely raw state or thinly disguised by superficial formal controls—useless rhetorical embellishment or specious logic. The poet corrects these abuses when instead of adding material she composes a setting for a poem's original impulse. She produces sonnets of conscious design into whose continuous mainstream she can assimilate new material. Even in the absence of a methodical device, she can sustain discourse, and she gains a control which she never enjoyed when her work was subject to the vagaries of a standard method. On their own modest scale, these poems are graceful, pleasing pieces. The next logical step—mobilizing the thought now that the poet commands material and form—damages some of her technical control, but this step brings her to the threshold of her poems of genuine stature.

CHAPTER SIX

THE INTEGRATED SONNETS

Greiffenberg does not achieve her fully integrated sonnets suddenly. These, too, are the product of a number of attempts. Here, however, the poet ascends not through a series of methods, but through a scale of quality. Her integrated sonnets are integrated in varying degrees. They are integrated to the extent that the poet has made thought, material, and the disposition of these two—form—all implicit in one another.

The most primitive of the integrated sonnets are organized according to a scheme. Their form is therefore inherent in neither the thought nor the material, and these, though they are compatible, are not indissolubly bound up in one another either. Next in quality are the sonnets whose arrangement is derived freely. The form is an intelligent and enlightening disposition of a poem's thought and material, but the sonnets fall short of full integration either because this disposition is not sustained over fourteen lines or because their material and idea do not combine into a new and inimitable whole. The fully integrated sonnets are the result of a perfect union of thought, material, and form.

The sonnets divide not only according to their quality, but also according to type, and type and quality are to some extent implicit in one another. The integrated sonnets may be argumentative, exclamatory, or generally descriptive. At once the crudest and the most complex of these types is the argumentative delivery. An argument may be either a transparent logical scheme which begs the question or a highly sophisticated disquisition which takes maximum advantage of thought, material, and form. An exclamation has a fairly regular prescribed format—the crescendo—which, like the argument, exercises some control over a sonnet's formal qualities. An exclamation, however, is not as rigorous as an argument. While it constrains the poet to be solicitous of the organization of her poem, it demands no subtle intellectual process. Descriptive delivery is less defined than either of the others. It binds the poet neither to rigorous thought nor to artful arrangement. She is, however, behoven to select her material with care.

The most primitive of the integrated poems are those which argue according to a prefabricated scheme. The scheme itself is a primitive argument, and the sponsorship of the case put forth in the poem devolves entirely upon this scheme. The scheme obviates any need for a judicious arrangement of thought and material. Since it states its case coercively, if not persuasively, it renders superfluous any effort to enlist the poem's tone or exploit the material in the interest of the argument.

In the weakest of these poems, the schemed argument extends over only two quatrains. Typically (sonnet 171 is an example), a poem begins with a negative formula: either a series of rhetorical questions which imply a negative response or a succession of statements in the negative. It then proceeds, usually in the second quatrain, to a positive rejoinder to or completion of the statement in the first quatrain. With the expiration of the "nicht . . . sondern" scheme in the second quatrain, the integrated portion of the poem is at an end. The sestet, to which the poet perforce must leap, is then pieced together from available scraps of thought and material.

The poems integrated on a scheme which covers fourteen lines enlarge this basic procedure, extending either the negative or the positive member of the argument across another strophe. The enlargement entails some formal considerations. A means of stretching one side of the argument must be found. Since, moreover, the positive and negative statements of the argument will occupy three strophes, the sonnet's fourth stanza must yet be disposed of. Neither task presents a major difficulty. The extended side of the argument need only be stated more and more emphatically, and the fourth strophe may amount to no more than a couplet, an apt space in which to summarize a two-sided debate. Sonnet 77, which is not included here, is such an instance; it extends the negative member of the argument.

A freely derived form determined solely by the needs and potentials of a poem's idea and material is a major step toward fully harmonious composition. The freely integrated sonnets begin modestly enough: only the two quatrains are integrated. The poems may be either descriptive or exclamatory. Descriptive delivery, which is neither bound by nor guided by the formal constraints characteristic of an exclamation, gives the poet more difficulty. Just this lack of external control may be responsible for the relatively large number of descriptive poems which she cannot integrate beyond the second quatrain. In sonnet 120 she has failed to sustain the controlled discourse even over eight lines. The poem breaks at line 7, but the integrated portion at its beginning is an especially beautiful meshing of idea and material. The poem belongs to a group of seven which separates the sonnets on the nativity from those which go on from Jesus' baptism to his ministry. Four of the pieces are reflections for New Year's Day, occasioned by the traditional belief that on this day Jesus was presented in the temple and received his name. Sonnet 120 is the last of these.

120
Andere Neu Jahrs Gedanken.

JEsu / meines Wunsches Ziel / mein Allwesendes Verlangen /
mein verneute Ewigkeit / und auch ewig neue Wonne /
meine Herz-umgebende / doch darinn aufgangne Sonne!
  wollst den immer-wärungs Lauff ietzund auf das neu' anfangen.
    Deine Gnade bleibet stät / ist nicht mit dem Jahr vergangen.
Eine Güt der andern folgt / wie an einer Rosen Krone
eine niegeendte Reih' geht aus Einem Strahlen Throne.
Herz-verlangter Wunder Glück / laß mich eines nur empfangen.
  Dich / mein allvergnügend Gut / wünsch und will ich einig haben.
  JEsu / schenk mir deine Gnade / mach es sonsten wie du wilt.
Ich (ach ein ungleicher Tausch /) nichts / vor aller Gaben Gaben /
  gib mich ganz und gar dir eigen. Ach verneu dein Himmel Bild!
  JEsu / rechter Wunderbar! sey es auch auf mein Begehren.
dieses Wunder-Stuck loßbrenn / dir zu unerhörten Ehren!

    The integrated portion of the poem consists of a long address to Jesus (lines 1-3), followed by a brief petition (line 4) and a short laudatory description (lines 5-7). In all of these the paradox of time and eternity is prominent. It is an especially appropriate turn of thought for the occasion: an address to a timeless God on that particular day which commemorates the temporality of human affairs. The motif emerges first slowly and then starkly. It is absent in the first epithet, which expresses only the poet's devotion, but colors the second, which describes this devotion as "Allwesend." The adjective may be construed either temporally or spatially: Jesus is always and constantly the poet's desire, or he is that desire which at any given moment occupies her whole awareness. Line 2 proceeds into sharp temporal paradoxes, plotting "neu" against "ewig" with chiastic interchange: Jesus' eternity is apprehended by the poet with periodic renewal and perpetually anew. The relationship between his nature as described here and her mode of apprehension is paradoxical. In keeping with this contradiction between man's temporality and God's timelessness—in keeping also with the contradiction that inheres in Jesus, who is both God and man—the poet's mode of apprehension is itself a paradox of duration and change: "ewig neu."

    Line 3 expresses the paradox spatially and introduces a symbol. Jesus is a sun which both surrounds the poet's heart and rises within it. Just as he is free of the laws governing time, he is independent of those which rule space. He is a light which both suffuses her and dwells within her. The sun is an ancient symbol of God and of eternity; this particular sun surrounds the poet's heart. The present participle calls attention to the shape of the sun: it is circular, and the circle, the geometric figure without beginning or end, is the symbol of eternity par excellence. Once it has been introduced into the poem in line 3, it dominates the remaining discussion of eternity. Line 4, a gentle request, no more than a reminder, follows naturally from the formulas of address. It, too, juxtaposes time and eternity much in the fashion of line 2: here at the beginning of the year, Jesus should begin anew his eternal course. The course is circular: one year after another into perpetuity.

The passage of praise which begins in line 5 contrasts time and eternity once more. As in line 4 the occasion for appealing to Jesus, the beginning of the new year, becomes a foil for his timelessness. Then the poet abandons the perplexing paradoxes of time and eternity in favor of a singularly beautiful representation of Jesus' constancy. "Krone" (line 6) is the equivalent of corolla, the ring of petals on a flower. The single "Strahlen Thron" (line 7) from which the "niegeendte Reih'" goes out is the yellow center of a rose, the stamens and pistil. The "Reih'" itself is both the succession of petals which spirals from this center and the succession of roses which will spring from the seeds in this center after this particular blossom has vanished. Jesus' blessings are said to follow one another like the petals on a rose—in endless succession, circuit upon circuit—and like the progeny of the rose—in endless succession, generation upon generation. "Krone," moreover, calls attention to the shape of the flower: it is circular. The poet has observed her rose with great care and found in it a second, extraordinarily delicately perceived double symbol of eternity.

Here the poem breaks. It turns from the description of God's grace to a second petition. The careful integration of its thought with its occasion is disturbed, for this second request is not necessarily germane to the new year. Still the poet might have succeeded in meshing the final movement with the opening strophes if she had fulfilled two conditions: if she had refined its thought into a continuous presentation, and if she had reconciled this thought with the poem's reflections on eternity and preserved some remnant of the original imagery. She has not refined the thought. It leaps from petition (lines 8-10) to a response to the fulfillment of the request (lines 11-12.1) and back again to petition (lines 12.2-14). The new year, time, and eternity have disappeared, as has the careful match of material and thought. The poet speaks plainly to the point of prosaism. Her two metaphors (lines 12 and 14), the one cosmic, the other incendiary, are matters of a moment. The piece concludes with an external reference to some specific miracle ("dieses Wunder-Stuck") for which the poem has laid no groundwork. The poet is not playing fair: she conceals essential information, and without this information her poem cannot maintain itself. A splendidly conceived occasional piece whose thought is entirely appropriate to its occasion, faultlessly integrated with compatible and illuminating material, and intelligently laid out in address, petition, and praise has been spoiled because its conception was not adequate for fourteen lines.

An exclamation, since it is by its very nature a fairly defined format for a poem, affords a broad basic outline for the arrangement of thought and material. Greiffenberg has little difficulty sustaining an exclamation over two quatrains. She can move directly into a crescendo, letting the pitch of her delivery rise steadily. In a span of eight lines the crescendo is unlikely to culminate prematurely, nor is the poet likely to exhaust her pertinent material. The two quatrains of sonnet 170, a burst of jubilation over the resurrection, are faultless.

170
[Auf die Frölich- und Herrliche Auferstehung Christi.]

ENgel! blaset die Trompeten! Seraphinen / singt und klingt /
Jubil-Jubil-Jubiliret / hoch-erfreuter Himmel-Chor!
Sonn' und Sterne / glänzt und danzet eurem Triumphirer vor!
Berg' und Hügel / Fels und Thürne / auch in frohen Jauchzen springt!
 ihr für alls beglückte Menschen / weil es euch zu Heil gelingt /
Lobet / Preiset / Ehret / Danket / und erhebet hoch empor
den / der sich und euch erhebet aus des Todts ins Himmels Chor.
Dann die Paradeisisch' Unschuld / sein' Erstehung / euch mitbringt.
 Solte wol die Sünden-Macht dessen Allmacht überstreben /
der die selbst' Unendlichkeit? nein sie muß sich ganz ergeben:
sein verdienstes-Meer kan löschen / nicht nur Fünklein / ganze Feur.
 Ach der lang verlangt' Erlöser tödtet alle ungeheur.
Was will Welt / Tod! Teuffel / Höll / einem Christen abgewinnen?
die sind ganz verstört / verheert: Dieser herrscht im Himmel drinnen.

The poem begins already at a high pitch: a command to the angels. It will climb higher yet, not because the poet is ascending the order of beings, obviously, but because her delivery becomes more and more pressing. Line 1 contains two imperatives; each occupies a halfline; both are addressed to beings of the highest order. The second halfline is onomatopoetic. The high, bright vowels in "singt und klingt" suggest the sounds of celestial music; their penetrating quality, redoubled in the rhyme, gives the command a special urgency. This urgency increases in the trebling of the stem syllables of the imperative verb in line 2. Because this stem is an intelligible fragment, the trebling effects also a semantic reinforcement, evoking *Jubel* as it invokes it. In line 3 compound imperatives begin. They reach maximum density in the quadruple summons of line 4, and resolve themselves momentarily in the simple verb at the end of the line.

Even while the urgency of her commands increases, the poet is descending a ladder of creation. She begins with the heavenly beings, proceeds to the celestial bodies, and from these to the towering structures on the earth. She is moving down to the principal object of her appeal, mankind, to which she devotes the entire second quatrain. Her full command occupies three lines, 5-7, which are the heart of the poem and the apex of the crescendo. The command is made copious by modifiers, and these modifiers capture the poem's central thought. In line 5 the poet explains why man is her primary object: he is foremost blessed by the occasion for this outburst of joy. "Es" in the second halfline of 5 is only a hint, an anacrusis as it were, to the crucial information which will follow ("gelingt" is equivalent to *gelangt*). Because line 5 is fragmentary, it flows swiftly into line 6, the most urgent and dense of the commands, an asyndetic series of four—and beyond the conjunction, five—synonyms for the expression of gratitude. The neutral "e" in the unstressed syllables and the identical suffixes on all the verbs throw their stems, which fall under the stresses of the line, into high relief. The rapid succession of equal rhythmic stresses enhances the effect of multitudinousness in the long series. The sense of the second halfline and, among the dark vowels, the bright one in the accented syllable of "erhebet" force the primary stress onto this word, the most important in the halfline and a second anticipation of an imminent climax. Because the strongly transitive verb lacks an object, the sentence rushes on into the completion of its sense and the culmination of the command in line 7. "Erhebet" becomes the key word: for the gratitude man owes God, for the resurrection of the Lord, and for mankind's release from death. With the conclusion of this long sentence, the tension generated by the suspension of its sense and by the growing urgency and density of the imperatives is released. Line 8 is a postscript, an ebbing away after the burst of power in the turgid syntax of lines 5-7.

As in all the sonnets which restrict the proper procedure of their composition to the octave, the sestet here is a task unto itself and a blemish to the poem. The problem which the poet raises in lines 9-10.1 is superfluous now that Christ is indeed risen and mankind delivered. The solution to the problem in the second halfline of 10 is self-evident. To fill two lines the poet has employed her technique for schematic argument: a rhetorical question which implies a negative response and then that response. Line 11 is equally feeble. With the exception of "verdienstes-Meer," the metaphoric words are merely quantitative, and the "ocean of merit" is qualitative only to the extent that "merit" gains from the compound the power to "extinguish." "Fünklein" and "Feur" are purely quantitative, one being simply a smaller portion of the other. The qualities of the two—brightness, heat—never come into play, and the words have no metaphoric referents.[1]

In the second tercet the poet recovers, launching into the praise and jubilation to which she summoned all creation in the octave. Here again she uses asyndetons to express her triumphant response to the resurrection, and she releases the turgor of the asyndetic series in the concluding

---

[1] If the reader is generous with the poet and gives her the benefit of the doubt, "Feur" at the end of line 11 can be said to refer to the fires of hell. This interpretation, however, borders on stock response. In the preceding lines the poet has not prepared the way for such an association. Lines 12-14, which clearly discuss the destruction of hell, belong to a new strophe. Only at a stretch can they be construed to furnish a setting for "Feur" at the end of the first tercet.

halfline's unpretentious expression. The first tercet, however, has done its damage. Only the octave of the sonnet is integrated.

The sonnets which are freely integrated over fourteen lines are within a hair's breadth of full integration. These poems are almost exclusively argumentative. They argue freely: they have no prefabricated scheme which bears the burden of the argument; rather, the thought itself must conduct the debate. This means that the thought must be perfectly clear. It must be presented in such a fashion that its very movement is a cogent argument. In these pieces the poet has refined her thought into a carefully controlled continuous and consistent delivery, and she maintains this delivery without serious lapse throughout the poem.

Sonnet 78, in the middle of the cycle on the thwarted trip, is a fine example of dialectical argument. The poem follows a sonnet in which the poet reconciles herself with God's mysterious ways. Here she submits to him and in doing so triumphs over herself and her misfortune.

78
Gänzliche Ergeb- und Begebung / in und nach Gottes Willen / in dieser und allen Sachen.

>   DEr Himmel ist gerecht. Möcht' auch mein Herz zerspringen
> vor Leid und Schmerzens Angst / noch gleichwol sag' ich frey /
> daß wunder Heiligkeit in seiner Schickung sey.
> Mir muß / will mir schon nicht mein Wunsch / sein Lob gelingen.
>   Will ihm den Siegs-Gesang / auch unterligend / singen:
> deñ sein Will hat gesiegt / und meiner fällt ihm bey.
> Mit ihm untrennlich Er soll bleiben einerley:
> kan überwunden so den Sieg auf mein Ort bringen.
>   Gehts ohne Schmerz nicht ab / geschichts nicht sonder Thränen:
> denk / daß du um so viel / mehr freuden Aehren kriegst.
> Das gegenwärtig man zu opfern muß gewähnen
>   der Künfftigkeit / das du hernach mit Lachē siegst.
> Mustu dich hier / mein Herz / der Tugend unterwerffen /
> ein kleines-dort wird dich nichts mehr betrüben dörffen.

The poem begins with a thesis: "Der Himmel ist gerecht." Not only does the statement hold for the particular situation into which it is introduced here and in which it will set off a chain of thought; in a Christian context it is also an objective truth. The argument opens on neutral ground. The second and third halflines introduce the first antithesis: the poet is pained and anxious. The second halfline of 2 and line 3 are a variation on the thesis, an example of heaven's competence which is placed now in specific and express relationship to the antithesis: despite her pain and anxiety, the poet advertently confesses the sanctity of the divine ordinance. The last line of the quatrain resolves the conflict in synthesis: the poet abandons her own desires, the genesis of her distress, in her acknowledgment of God.

In the second quatrain this synthesis springs apart again. Line 5 reduces the content of the first quatrain to a single line. It elevates "Lob" in line 4 to "Siegs-Gesang" and reduces the poet's abandonment of her wish to a state of defeat ("unterligen"). The two are antithetical. This second antithesis is quickly resolved. In line 6 the poet goes a step beyond abandoning her own wishes; she admits God's victory and unites her will with his. Line 7 underscores this second synthesis by repeating it emphatically. Line 8 produces a third antithesis and leaves the octave open and unresolved: the defeat which the poet has described on lines 5-6 will become her victory.

The sestet dwells on this one antithesis, defining it more clearly in successive reformulations, until it becomes entirely precise and, because of this precision, resolved. As is commonly the case in the integrated sonnets, this final six-line movement divides into a four-line strophe and a concluding couplet. To call this four-line strophe a third quatrain is misleading,[2] because it is not the last of a group of three quatrains, but rather the first of an asymmetrical sestet. This is not an English sonnet; it is an unorthodoxly divided sonnet in the continental manner. The division into a four-line and a two-line strophe is effected here by the rhyme scheme and, more pertinently, by an antonymic brace. "Thränen" at the end of line 9 finds a response in "Lachen" toward the end of line 12, and this echo holds the four lines together. But for this correspondence, the sestet would fall into three groups of two, for each pair of lines rephrases the antithesis in line 8. Lines 9-10 are little more than an expansion and thus a slackening of the terse riddle at the end of the octave. The counterpoise of "Schmerz" and "freuden" is studiedly unenlightening; "Aehren" is a meaningless word. The juxtaposition of "gegenwärtig" and "Künfftigkeit" in lines 11-12 is somewhat more informative, setting the places of defeat and victory apart temporally. The matter becomes entirely clear, and the antithesis resolves itself, when lines 13-14 stipulate that the one is "hier," the other "dort." These adverbs, like *diesseits* and *jenseits* without further context, are unambiguous, the more so since the poet's prospective experience "dort" (line 14) is plainly what she expects of the hereafter. "Ein kleines-dort" is probably a printer's error. The line should read: "ein kleines: dort wird dich nichts mehr betrüben dörffen." The caesura moves forward, so that the rhythm of speech and the sense of the line correspond. "Ein kleines" may be equivalent to *eine Kleinigkeit,* which would refer to the state of affairs described in line 13, or it may be the old adverbial usage

---

[2] See Horst-Joachim Frank, "Catherina Regina von Greiffenberg: Untersuchungen zu ihrer Persönlichkeit und Sonettdichtung" (Diss. Hamburg, 1958), pp. 274-82. Frank's elaborate statistical summary of the division of Greiffenberg's sonnets must be regarded with caution. His criteria for determining the breaks in the poems appear to have been punctuation and rhyme scheme. The organization of a sonnet, however, is a more subtle question. It involves the poem's logic, its imagery and other rhetorical figures, its tone—and these need not be reflected in punctuation and rhyme scheme.

which the Luther Bible has made familiar. It is rendered in the King James version as "a little while."[3]

Even though Greiffenberg has succeeded here in sustaining the discourse across fourteen lines, the octave is of markedly better quality than the sestet. It is always logical, always lucid; the thought grows continuously; no word is wasted. The sestet is marred by a dilatory tactic: thought is suspended as the poet carefully withholds and then divulges information. Clearly she has expended the better part of her effort in the two quatrains. She salvages the sestet by means of a clever ploy and an intriguing turn of thought at the end of the octave. Line 8 generates a suspense which saves the six subsequent lines from superfluousness.

All three types of delivery—descriptive, exclamatory, and argumentative—are represented in the fully integrated sonnets. The descriptive poems are distinguished by the poet's control of her material, which she selects and arranges with a sure hand and a keen sense for delicate evocation. Greiffenberg turns the exclamatory sonnets into unique displays of her power to manipulate words and levels of tone. The argumentative sonnets, with their exacting demands upon thought and logic, are the most challenging of the lot. Because an argument gains much if it appeals to the emotions and to the imagination as well as to the intellect, these pieces are the poet's best opportunity fully to integrate thought, material, and form.

In each group of poems Greiffenberg both observes and disregards the orthodox division of the sonnet. Because the organization of these poems is no accident—because the poet is in full control and may arrange her piece as she pleases—it is possible to examine here the effect of the various divisions and to draw conclusions about the competence of the traditional format of the sonnet. Significantly, Greiffenberg takes her greatest liberties in the descriptive poems, which by their very nature imply no prescribed delivery. In the exclamatory sonnets she is somewhat more conservative, and in the argumentative pieces she is very much disposed to divide a poem into two quatrains and two tercets. In her small aberrations the exact function of the conventional divisions defines itself clearly, for an argument and an orthodox sonnet are indigenously compatible.

Greiffenberg has produced three particularly fine fully integrated descriptive sonnets. All are poised and graceful without the least pretentiousness. Two are unorthodox compositions with irregular meter and unconventional division of the fourteen lines. The third is a more

---

[3] Luther uses "ein kleines" in conjunction with a preposition or an adverb. John 16, 16: "Über ein kleines, so werdet ihr mich nicht sehen; und aber über ein kleines, so werdet ihr mich sehen"; Haggai 2, 6: "Es ist noch ein kleines dahin. . . ." *Deutsches Wörterbuch* cites also examples of "ein kleines" alone as a temporal adverb. Other obscurities in the poem: "sonder" = *ohne* (Line 9); "gewähnen" = *gewöhnen* (line 11).

regular sonnet. Sonnet 210, in the miscellaneous group at the beginning of the final fifty in the collection, is the best of the poems for a new year. The elaborate title—"Als mir einmal / am H. Drey König Abend / beym Eyrgiessen / der HErr Christus am Creutz klar und natürlich erschienen / oder aufgefahren"—describes the occasion and the context of the poem: the poet is pouring eggs on the evening of Epiphany, as it is customary elsewhere in the German-speaking countries to pour molten lead into water on New Year's Eve.[4] The sonnet is devoted entirely to weighing three possible auguries of the crucifix which has appeared. Each of the auguries occupies a quatrain, and all are cast under the sign of the poet's trust in God, which is advanced in the opening statement of the poem, cited again in line 13, and defended in an etymological proof in the final line. The material—the three possible interpretations of the omen—the arrangement of the material into three symmetrical strophes, and the delivery of the material in an unaffected tone of tranquil confidence which reflects the opening and concluding statements of trust constitute a simple and unusually moving poem.

Sonnet 110 is the finest of the nativity sonnets. Like most of the other poems in the group, it works with the paradoxes of the miraculous birth. It owes its superiority to the selection and the arrangement of the material for these paradoxes.

110
[Auf [Christi] Mensch-werdige Wunder-That.]

    DEr selbselbste Lebens-Safft / wird mit Milch getränket.
Der die weite Welt besiegt /
in der ängen Krippen ligt.
Wunder! aller Himmel HErr sich der Erden schenket.
    Der selbst ist das Höchste Gut / sich ins Elend senket.
Die Bewegung wird gewiegt:
von der selbst der Himmel kriegt
seines Lauffes Ordnung-Pflicht / und nach ihr sich lenket.
    Hirten! lasst den Himmel stehn /
und uns in den Stall hingehn!
kam' euch jemals auch zu Ohren
    solch ein sonder-Wunderwerk /
daß die Schwachheit hat die Stärk'
und ein Stern die Sonn gebohren?

The conspicuous difference between this poem and the others in the group is that sonnet 110 is concrete and coherent, the paradoxes notwithstanding. The poet has before her a visible scene, and she chooses paradoxes which refer to this scene: an infant receives milk, lies in a manger, is rocked. The paradoxes are less a cerebral exercise in coun-

---

[4] See Frank, "Greiffenberg" (Diss.), p. 187.

terpoised abstractions than the representation of a manifest miracle.

The paradoxes also hang together formally. The lines are not succinct units; rather the combination of long and short lines means that a strophe must be whole before the asymmetrical lines become a symmetrical unit, before the pattern into which they are arranged makes sense. The irregular meter itself promotes the wholeness of the strophes. Because of the metrical contrast between the long and the short lines, the short lines flow rapidly into one another, and their junction is promoted by enjambement. Even the long lines are asymmetrical, consisting of halflines of four and three stresses respectively. The abbreviated second halfline never reaches full metrical repose, and the strophe moves easily into the short lines and rapidly across these. The preponderance of one- and two-syllable words protects the fluency of the rhythm. Finally, the rhyme word of the quatrain's first line is unusually audible over the short lines and calls for its resolution in the last line of a quatrain.

The quatrains, then, cohere materially insofar as their paradoxes contribute to a description of the scene in the stable, and formally. Material coherence is more pronounced in the first strophe, where only the last line is abstract. In the second only line 6 is concrete. Line 5, an oblique paradox, is altogether abstract, and the relative clause in lines 7-8, which as a syntactically subordinate unit coheres to line 6, forsakes the stable for the cosmos. The poet has exhausted her material on the scene in the stable.

She moves boldly to another, which she presents with vivid dramatic immediacy. She delivers a blunt imperative: "Hirten! lasst den Himmel stehn." The abrupt order to persons whom the poet takes entirely seriously conjures up a famous landscape of the Christian tradition: shepherds standing on a hillside staring amazed into the night sky from which the angels have just departed. The poet then returns attention to the scene in the stable. The setting, however, does not change again. The poet remains with the shepherds on the hillside and describes to them what they are to see. The dramatic situation gives the description a concrete setting. The graceful phrasing with continuous enjambement, assonance, and alliteration furnish it with formal coherence. The description itself is purest abstraction, unadulterated miraculousness. Even the metaphor of star and sun is more ethereal than material in its unblemished luminousness.

The sonnet divides very unorthodoxly. Lines 9 and 10, which rhyme as a couplet, are indeed a two-line strophe at the end of the octave. This irregularity does not damage the piece seriously. One reason is that the break between lines 10 and 11 is gentle. All six concluding lines belong to an address to the shepherds. The other reason is more fundamental to the poem: while it does not exploit the sonnet form to full advantage, neither does it depend heavily upon the best possibilities of this form. The poem is neither an exclamation nor an argument, both of which require that the poet compose a carefully arranged continuous presentation, nor does it describe a continuous event. Like sonnet 210, which profits similarly from regular patterns of irregular meter, sonnet 110 illuminates various spots on a given scene. It need not have been a sonnet. It hardly is—and in only one respect is it the worse for it: sonnet 110 is not a statuesque piece. Like sonnet 210, it is more endearing than imposing.

Sonnet 122, on the other hand, is not endearing. In this first of a group on the miracles Jesus performed, the poet recounts the stilling of the tempest.

122

Uber des Allwachenden Schlaf / in dem Wind-bestürmten Schifflein.

GOTT schläfft / und schläfft doch nicht. Er schläffet / zu entdecken
der Jünger Glaubens-Schwäch' im Wetter-Widerstand /
wañ er von ihnen zieht die Stürme-Schirmungs-Hand;
will / nach dem schein / den Schein des Gnaden-Augs verstecken.
   der strengen Noht Gebot / macht ihn behend erwecken.
Er / der die Wind verbindt / hat an der Hand das Band /
kan wider ruffen bald / die so Er ausgesandt:
sie stellen sich stracks ein aus allen Felsen-Ecken.
   Die Welle / die sich mit der hohen Wolken wolt
vermählen / welche sich herunter neigen solt /
ist wider in den Grund / zum Ordnungs Ort / gewichen.
   Nun Meer und Wind wird still / ein hohe Frag geht an:
was ist / dem Wind und Meer gehorchen / vor ein Mann?
ich antwort': eben der / der GOtt und uns verglichen.

From the accounts in the first three gospels (Matthew 8, 23-27; Mark 4, 35-41; Luke 8, 22-25) the poet selects the material which is pertinent to her purpose and arranges it within fourteen lines, condensing or expanding it according to her needs. She reduces the biblical accounts of the incident to four constituent events; to each she devotes one strophe. Like Luke, she begins with Jesus' sleep, upon which she enlarges with commentary. The commentary converts the biblical description of the storm and Jesus' reproach to the apostles, which the poet elides as an event, into a preliminary interpretation of the story as a test of the apostles' faith. The commentary endows the poem with a purpose beyond pure narration and obviates the need for a moralizing conclusion. It changes the storm, however, into a pale copy of itself. "Wetter-Widerstand" in line 2 and "Stürme-Schirmungs-Hand" in line 3 are something less than vivid evocations of a tempest. They condense what is in Luke a lively description to hypertrophied concepts distinguished only by the mental gymnastics they entail. Like the alliteration in the compounds, the pun on "Schein" in line 4 is unproductive. The first quatrain, then, recounts but one event: "Gott schläfft."

The second quatrain reduces and expands in a similar fashion. Here, however, two events are recounted: Jesus awakens (line 5) and the storm subsides (line 8). Omitted are the apostles' alarm and their appeal to the master, and Jesus' remonstrance to the tempest. This is absorbed into the commentary (lines 6-7) and rendered into a skillfully executed aside on Jesus' divinity. The etymological figure "verbindt . . . Band" is not a gratuitous embellishment but a semantic proof. The internal rhyme "Wind verbindt" in no way compromises the sense of the line.

To this point the account of the episode has been very spare indeed: one metrical foot in the first quatrain, two lines in the second. The first tercet takes up the event described in line 8 and converts this summary rendition of the turning point of the story into the climax of the poem. The storm, which heretofore has entered only obliquely into the commentary, at last appears. For the first time the poet waxes florid, describing at her own invention and in a single sentence which embraces two relative clauses the restoration of order from turmoil. It is a purple patch: an elegant display of perfectly controlled syntax and continuous assonance and alliteration.

Spare expression returns in the second tercet. The poet assumes the astonishment of the apostles and elides it. Telescoping the narrative handily, she moves immediately to the question about Jesus' identity, which she reduces to a single line. In the final line, she responds to the question, casting her brief and sparsely told tale into the context of Christian redemption.

The sonnet divides with perfect orthodoxy. With interpretive elaborations, the quatrains recount a story up to its turning point. The first tercet takes up this turning point and describes it in detail—by virtue of both its content and its expression it is the high point of the poem. The second tercet brings a denouement which throws the story into a larger context. For all its unevenness—the poet hits her stride only in the first tercet—sonnet 122 enjoys that certain dignity and stature which inheres in an orthodox sonnet. It is a characteristic which is particularly promising in a presentation that requires an especial rigor.

As a moderately rigorous procedure, exclamatory delivery illuminates the competence of the orthodox sonnet more precisely. The basic format of the exclamation—the crescendo—is uncomplicated over a space of eight lines: the tone can simply rise steadily, as in the quatrains of sonnet 120. Maintaining an exclamatory delivery over fourteen lines is a complex undertaking. The levels of tone must be carefully arranged within the prescribed space, and this arrangement calls into play those peculiar characteristics which have made a sonnet a distinctive form. The collection offers three fine exclamatory poems: sonnets 129, 225, and 229. Sonnets 129 and 229 are virtuoso pieces. The latter, one of fifteen entitled "GOtt-lobende Frülings-Lust," consists of a single carefully organized, though erratically subdivided sentence which is full of assonance, alliteration, and internal rhyme. The former, which concludes the group of eight on Jesus' miracles, is divided, like many of Greiffenberg's lesser sonnets, into three quatrains in sequence and a concluding couplet.

129
Auf unsers Heilandes Allmacht-durchstrahlten Wunder-Wandel auf dieser Erden.

JEsu! deine Wunder / wundern und bestürzen mich so sehr/
das ich / stummer / als der Stumm' / eh du ihm die Sprach gegeben /
steh' im zweiffel / welches ich zu erhebē an-soll' hebē.
Ja / sie mehren in den Händen / leitend sie / sich mehr und mehr.
　Lauter sonder-Seltenheiten sih' ich / wo ich mich hinkehr:
höre / was sonst unerhört / die gestorbenen beleben;
Blinden / das Gesicht und Liecht / Seelen-Sonn und Wonn darneben /
geben / gleicher weiß den Tauben das Gehör / zu Gottes Ehr.
　Krumme / lauffen wie die Reh auf der Allbewegung lenken.
auch der Aussatz lässt den Platz / deine Allmacht macht ihn rein.
Keine Sach' unüberwindlich /soll man / dir zu seyn / gedenken.
　Du beherrschest alles / alles muß dir Dienst-gehorsam seyn.
Doch in dem so über-Mild du dein Herz uns pflegst zuschenken:
zeigest / daß dir könne gleichen deine grosse Güt' allein.

The poem is an astonishing tour de force of figurae etymologicae, internal rhyme, assonance, and alliteration—all achieved without serious compromise of sense, syntax, or of the appointed rhythm of the poem's organization. The first quatrain is a balanced introduction to an outburst of praise. In tones of anticipatory enthusiasm, the poet deliberates which of Jesus' miracles she should exalt. Lines 1-3 are a single sentence of sustained exclamatory force, enlarged in line 2 by a parenthetical insertion which preserves without fault the characteristic feature of the passage: paronomasia involving two crucial words in each line. This self-imposed limitation on the word play has two advantages: it enables the poet to sustain the device at length, and it controls the device so that the device never usurps the sense. The full stop at the end of line 3 curtails the unrelenting thrust of the sentence. Quite properly, the last line of the quatrain is an additional remark which does not renew this urgent advance. Here for the first time paronomasia falls also upon a word which does not constitute the basic sense of a phrase, but only embellishes it.

The force of the delivery mounts again in the first one and one-half lines of the second quatrain. Clearly they anticipate an enumeration, preparing the way for a burst of praise which occupies the rest of the strophe. In this outburst the full force of the delivery is unleashed. It increases steadily throughout line 7, spurred by the battery of four direct objects with two internal rhymes and a threefold alliterative "s," and gains such momentum that the line spills over into 8 with a word which, startlingly, reproduces the previous end rhyme. In the last line of this quatrain, too, the tone diminishes. Here, as in line 4, the verbal figure involves a word which merely supplements the sense of the line.

Because the cadence of the catalogue descends to repose at the end of the second quatrain, it is a mistake to resume the enumeration in a third quatrain. The main force of the delivery is spent. Spent also are the best puns, rhymes, assonances, even the strongest expressions. After the dense juxtaposition of antonyms in line 6.2-8, the first halfline of 9 is not an idiom, but a cliché; line 9.2 is an addendum which does not greatly enrich the sense—this stipulation was clear though entirely implicit in the second quatrain—nor is it an auditory embellishment. In line 10 the poet strains to produce an internal rhyme and a pun. Her expression here is not merely stereotype; it is weak. The catalogue has reached the point of exhaustion, and lines 11-12 go over into a summary of its import.

Since the catalogue, the main thrust of the poem, is now concluded and wrapped up, the couplet is a difficulty. The poet extracts herself from it fairly gracefully. She refrains from appending an entirely new problem and solving it promptly. Instead she adduces a second facet to the omnipotence described in lines 11-12. That Greiffenberg conceives of God's benevolence and his omnipotence as complementary qualities is clear in sonnet 35, especially lines 10-11, and in sonnet 130. Here she goes on in line 13 to submit that Jesus accompanies his miracles with a specific gesture of tender devotion—a gesture which is not substantiated in the foregoing outburst over his miracles—and from this gesture she draws conclusions on his essential nature. As in sonnets 35 and 130, she concludes that benevolence is God's dominant quality.

Sonnet 129 is an amazing display of the poet's power to manipulate words into special effects without damaging the sense of her expression or the organization of her delivery. She has laid the poem out into three quatrains and a couplet. The first quatrain is a prelude to the principal thrust of the poem, which will come forward in the second. In line 4 the tone of the delivery moderates, preparatory to a swift intensification in lines 5-7. Line 7 is the high point of this strophe and, as it turns out, of the poem, for after the diminuendo in line 8, the poet is unable to restore the tone to its previous level. Her chosen organization becomes a stumbling block. Since the couplet of a sonnet laid out in this fashion is obviously the proper place for a conclusion, the organization of the poem requires that the burst of praise, which takes the form of a catalogue, be maintained over two quatrains. To preserve a catalogue of such urgent tone and distinctive expression throughout eight lines is exceedingly difficult. Inevitably it deteriorates; that it expires altogether in line 10 is not surprising. Under the circumstances, the poet has cut her losses with fair skill.

Even if she had maintained the initial quality of her presentation—if the catalogue following the introductory quatrain had run faultlessly over two more quatrains and a pertinent couplet had concluded the poem—Greiffenberg would have achieved in sonnet 129 an entirely different effect from that of sonnet 225, a less spectacular, but more subtly organized piece. Because the poem resembles sonnet 170 (see above, pp. 76-78), a comparison of the two is revealing of Greiffenberg's measures to maintain an exclamation at length.

225
GOtt-lobende Frülings-Lust.

JAuchzet / Bäume / Vögel singet! danzet / Blumen / Felder lacht!
springt / ihr Brünnlein! Bächlein rauscht! spielet ihr gelinden Winde!
walle / Lust-bewegtes Träid! süsse Flüsse fliest geschwinde!
opffert Lob-Geruch dem Schöpffer / der euch frisch und neu gemacht!
 jedes Blühlein sey ein Schale / drauff Lob-Opffer ihm gebracht /
jedes Gräslein eine Seul / da sein Namens-Ehr man finde.
an die neu-belaubten Aestlein / GOttes Gnaden-Ruhm man binde!
daß / so weit sein Güt sich strecket / werd' auch seiner Ehr gedacht.
 Du vor alles / Menschen Volck / seiner Güte Einfluß Ziele!
aller Lieblichkeit Genießer; Abgrund / wo der Wunderfluß
endet uñ zu gut verwendet seinē Lieb-vergultē Guß.
 GOtt mit Herz / Hand / Sinn und Stimm / lobe / preiße / dicht' und spiele.
Laß / vor Lieb' und Lobes-Gier / Muht und Blut zu Kohlen werden /
lege Lob und Dank darauff: Gott zum süssen Rauch auf Erden.

Sonnet 170 built up rapidly to a point of culmination in lines 6-7. Sonnet 225 moves slowly to a climax, reserving its highest point to line 14. The poet's means of withholding the crescendo are apparent already in the first quatrain. Instead of ascending immediately to a high pitch of excitement, she very gradually diminishes the urgency of the commands. She begins with four imperatives in a single line. The verbs and the nouns of address are twice interchanged chiastically. Each halfline begins and ends with a verb, so that the extremes of each are active, the middle stable. These kinetic extremes draw the halfline taut. Since the two halflines are balanced against one another, however, the total structure is stable. The energy of the halflines is contained; it remains potential. Consequently the first line of the poem is tense with restrained motion.

The tension begins to ease in line 2. Here there are only three imperatives. The line is not only less full than line 1; it is also not balanced. It can flow freely forward. The poet, moreover, becomes expansive. She replaces the Spartan frugality of the first line's expression with less astringent diction, permitting herself the luxury of an adjective in the second halfline, which, in consequence of this and of the personal pronoun, comprises only one imperative. The redoubling in "gelinden Winde" of a vowel prolonged by a nasal slows the rapid flow of syllables. The line ends on an unstressed syllable. Conventional metrical terminology notwithstanding (*stress, unstress* is traditionally called "falling rhythm"), the line is at its conclusion rhythmically on the uptake and therefore unstable.[5] The contrast between its unstressed final syllable and the stressed conclusion of line 1 enhances the instability, as does its general rhythmic fluidity, which contrasts with the first line's balanced containment. Because of this instability, the second line proceeds the more easily into the third.

Here the expression is more expansive yet. The line contains only two imperatives. These are interlaced with polysyllabic adjectives and an adverb. The tautness in line 1 is slackened completely in line 4, which contains but a single command. The command appears without a vocative. It consists entirely in the verb, which, however, is transitive and therefore incomplete without an object. This smallest unit of sense, the verb and its object, is embellished moreover by an indirect object, and the indirect object entails in turn a relative clause. The poet is expatiating. The expression is relaxed.

The superb formal effect of this slow decrescendo is blemished slightly by a superfluous word in line 4. "Geruch," which in conjunction with "opffern" turns "Lob" into a burnt offering, has no counterpart in the tributes the poet requests of nature. Even if "Geruch" is taken to mean natural scents, it corresponds only sporadically with the tribute—with that of the "Blumen" and "Winde," conceivably with that of the "Bäume" and "Träid" (= *Getreide*), hardly with that of the "Brünnlein," "Bächlein," and "Flüsse," and in no event with that of the "Vögel." The great virtue, with respect to sense, of the tribute requested is that in each instance the poet requires only that something be itself, enact its essential nature. Even the metaphoric verbs, with the possible exception of "jauchzet Bäume," describe actions which are accepted in the literary tradition as the enactment of the essential nature of the thing in question—for example, "Felder lacht." The philosophical implication—an enchanting concept—is that the very existence of these things is praise of God. In sonnet 223, lines 10-12, Greiffenberg describes the concept at length: "des ganzen Wesen Werk"—the essential mechanism (= "Werk") of the whole foregoing allegory on the coming of spring—

---

[5] The vocal inflection of a final unstressed syllable in poetry is not unlike the usual inflection on the last syllable of a yes-or-no question in normal speech. The resemblance can be heard clearly when the effect of an unstressed final syllable is compared with that of a stressed final syllable, which is similar to the usual vocal inflection of a declarative sentence. A yes-or-no question is clearly an open form, in need of completion in a reply. This same tone of tentativeness colors the effect of an unstressed final syllable in prosody. The phenomenon, of course, is relative, not absolute. Rythmic effects in poetry, like auditory effects, depend upon both sound and sense, upon patterns of contrast and similarity, on countless devices at the disposal of the poet—and, not least, upon the suggestibility of the reader. In the last analysis, the tentative tone of a final unstressed syllable is a matter of real potential, not of fact.

[ist] Jubel Lob-Geschrey /
der Athem aller Ding / so nun aufs neue neu /
die durch die frische Lufft still-lautes Lob ihm geben.

The second quatrain is a plateau between the descending tone of the first strophe and the ascent which begins in the sestet. In the even tone of descriptive delivery the poet presents a spring festival in God's honor. The imagery of lines 5 and 6, particularly "Seul" in line 6, is faintly suggestive of the triumphal celebrations of Roman antiquity, which is the material for the allegory in sonnet 223. The poet does not pursue the matter, however, and the metaphoric implications are never fully realized. They are hampered also by the unpretentious tone of the presentation. No grandiose gesture, no linguistic pomp and circumstance fosters an evocation of Roman splendor. On the contrary, the prevalent diminutives, which become conspicuous in the simple syntax, color the expression with affectionate tenderness. More germane to the context in which the metaphors appear is that they transform a sensual similitude into a laudatory function. The flower, shaped like a bowl, becomes a sacrificial vessel; the straight and slender blade of grass is made to function as a triumphal column. Again the very existence of the things in nature is praise of God. The material of the metaphor in line 7, on the other hand, is germane. It refers to the trimming of the May tree in European spring festivals.[6] Line 8, a clause of purpose, is a summary statement for both quatrains and the end of the poem's first long movement.

In sestet the tension begins to mount again. The long and elaborate address to mankind retards the completion of the sentence, generating a mild suspense. As in sonnet 170, the preliminaries of the imperative verbs justify the prominence accorded mankind in the economy of the poem. Here, however, the second quatrain, which extends the competence of the first while it holds the poem's tone at an even level, has removed this approach to the high point of the sonnet to the sestet. The poet has organized her delivery in a manner which takes cognizance of the full format of a sonnet, and the poem is all of a piece.

The division of the sestet is somewhat problematic. The rhyme scheme would indicate that it consists of a four-line strophe and a couplet. The punctuation neither supports nor refutes this possibility. Though a colon at the end of line 11 would reflect the syntax more accurately than the full stop in the printed text, this emendation is not indicative of the correct division of the lines: a strophe can end as gracefully with a colon as with a period. Even the sense and the rhythm of the lines are an inconclusive indication. Line 9-11 obviously belong together: they constitute an elaborate preliminary address. Lines 12-14 are all imperatives, and yet lines 13-14 cohere more closely, since they

---

[6] Theodor H. Gaster, ed., *The New Golden Bough* (New York: 1959), pp. 80-83.

contain two imperatives in sequence and belong to one extended metaphor. On the balance of indications, however, a division between the formulas of address and the imperatives themselves would appear to be the more intelligent arrangement.

The second tercet would consist then of a double culmination to the poem. Line 12, the long-awaited predicate to the mounting vocative epithets in lines 9-11, is the first high point. It is a dense imperative of turgid syntax: a versus rapportatus of four members. It is promptly trumped in line 13, whose drastic incendiary metaphor is made the more grandiose by the sonorous solemnity of the long dark vowels in the second halfline. Line 13 is only a beginning: the first halfline of 14 supersedes it instantly. The adverbial "darauff" is indicative; it signifies the ascendancy of the final line. For its sake the poet has released her control over the metaphor. Grateful man is no longer simply inflamed with enthusiasm; he has become a sacrificial fire on which he is expected yet to heap an offering. The sense is distorted, but the form is preserved.

The poem is a meticulously organized and highly sophisticated exclamatory sonnet. It divides into two large movements, which complement one another. The octave is a subtle decrescendo, which reaches its low point at the end of the first quatrain. The second quatrain develops the idea of the first and maintains an even tone. The sestet is a crescendo, gradual in the first tercet and rapid in the second. The contours of the two movements are carefully drawn, and the force of the delivery judiciously distributed within them. Neither movement is excessively long. Each has its own purposefully placed high point. The two movements, moreover, are poised one against the other. The shorter, lighter sestet responds to the massiveness of the octave with the magnitude of its thought and the urgency of its delivery. The peak of the crescendo in the first half of line 14 is the pinnacle of the poem. The second halfline dips gently. Thus the poem's two long movements constitute an indissoluble whole, and this whole is a nearly perfect sonnet.

The full competence of the orthodox sonnet—its capacity to render an intellectual process with superb grace, clarity, and poise—defines itself precisely in the rigorous progress of argumentative delivery. Two of Greiffenberg's sonnets are pure and fully integrated arguments. Sonnet 9 is the second last of the poems on praise at the beginning of the collection. It is a meticulously executed dialectical argument, a faultless arrangement of thesis, antithesis, and synthesis in fourteen lines. Sonnet 34, the first of the poems requesting God's help in the poet's mysterious undertaking,[7] is a more monumental but less perfect piece. It stumbles at the end of the second quatrain, and the fault seriously disturbs the grace of the argument. A comparison of the two, beginning with the simpler, but more perfect poem, will illustrate the consequences of the blunder.

[7] See above, p. 15 and n. 27.

9
Demütiger Entschluß / GOtt zu loben.

 WAs fang' ich an? was untersteh' ich mich /
das höchste Werk auf Erden zuverrichten?
mein schlechtes Lob wird ihn vielmehr vernichten.
Er ist und bleibt / der Höchst geehrt für sich.
 Fahr fort / mein' Hand / preiß GOtt auch inniglich;
befleiße dich / sein Wunder-Lob zu dichten!
Du wirst dadurch zu mehrerm ihn verpflichten /
daß Er mit Freud auch wunderseeligt dich.
 Laß Lob / Ruhm / Preiß / zu wett den Engeln / klingen
mit Lust: ists schon so Heilig lieblich nicht /
und nicht so hoch / noch mit solch hellem Liecht:
 GOtt weiß doch wol / daß sich nicht gleich kan schwingen
die kleine Schwalb dem Adler: Ihm beliebt /
was treu gemeint / ob es schon schlecht verübt.

The quatrains are given over to thesis and antithesis. The strophes are counterpoised not only by virtue of their content, but also formally. Each has its own high point in the third line of the quatrain. The first ascends through three questions to this culmination,[8] the second over three imperatives. In both strophes the first two sentences each occupy a halfline, the third a full line. The mounting tension emanates in the first quatrain from the questions themselves: they circumscribe something which has not yet been defined. The word "Lob" in line 3 supplies the awaited information, and the line itself is the thesis. Line 4 elaborates; it lies on a descending plane. The imperatives in the second quatrain generate suspense because they contradict the thesis in the first strophe while the reason for the contradiction is still outstanding. The explanation appears in line 7, which is the antithesis. A word play reinforces the correspondence of lines 3 and 7: "mehreres" here refutes "vernichten" above. Again the last line of the quatrain elaborates, and the forward thrust subsides momentarily.

---

[8] If this reading is correct, the virgule at the end of line 1 should be replaced by a question mark. Alternatively, lines 1.2 -2 may be read as a single sentence, in which case "was" is equivalent to *wieso*. Admittedly, my interpretation runs against the text as it stands. I retain it for three reasons. Printer's errors, especially in punctuation, are not rare in the collection (see, for example, the virgule at the end of the last line of sonnet 188). Furthermore, two short queries followed by a yes-or-no question preserve a desirable tension in the passage, particularly in the steadily rising intonation of line 2, which would then build properly to the disclosure in line 3. Finally, if line 2 is read as a yes-or-no question, one of the major stresses of the sentence falls within "das höchste Werk auf Erden." This phrase is the salient point from which line 3 follows. If lines 1.2-2 are read as a single sentence, the phrase carries only secondary stresses, and "Lob" in line 3 loses much of its impact.

In the identically constructed quatrains the delivery has built up over three lines and descended in one. The sestet mounts upward over three and into the fourth, attaining the pinnacle of the poem in line 12. The first tercet, then, climbs steadily. It begins with a recapitulation of the antithesis. In the asyndeton of three direct objects in the first halfline of 9 the urgency begins to grow, rising through higher and higher vowel sounds until, after a brief dip at the beginning of the second halfline, it reaches high "i" at the end of the line. As if it were too rapidly propelled to stop here, the sentence spills over into line 10. It is made the more full, the more urgent by the adjacent rhythmic stresses on the three members of the asyndeton, which as equivalent units deserve equal emphasis. In line 10 begins one of the most suspenseful of syntactical forms: a concessive clause, which continues without pause to the end of line 11. Again a series augments the tension—the three negative qualifications of the concession, made pressingly urgent by overwhelming spirance. The concession takes account of the thesis. The problem posed in the first quatrain was not a strawman to be toppled at an appointed place, but a genuine difficulty reconfirmed here before being integrated into its antithesis. The concession remains open at the end of the tercet, raising the suspense to the point of poignancy.

The release begins in line 12, the point of synthesis which explains the compatibility of thesis and antithesis. It is a slow release, retarded by the displacement into line 13 of the subject and an object of the clause which begins in the second half of line 12. The conclusion to the concessive clause not only resolves the concession syntactically and logically; its material is also a response. By way of illustration, the conclusion invokes for its own purposes the emblem of the soaring eagle which carries the weaker wren (or swallow) on its back.[9] The swallow represents the poet; the eagle replaces the angels (line 9), to whom the poet cannot attain with her praise. The eagle is an emblematic counterpart to "hoch" and "Liecht" in line 11, for its fabled qualities are also that it can ascend into the sun or stare into the sun without harm.[10] The last sentence, which begins at the end of line 13, restates and elaborates the synthesis, clarifying it as a resolution of the conflict between thesis and antithesis.

Like the quatrains, the tercets are identical in their internal forms, but in inverted mirror image. The opening sentence in the first tercet runs over by two syllables into line 10. Similarly, the last sentence of the second tercet begins with three syllables at the end of line 13. The effect is more than formalistic symmetry. Because of the consequent enjambements, the colon at the end of line 11, at the height of the suspense, becomes the only long pause in the sestet. The concession and

---

[9] Arthur Henkel and Albrecht Schöne, *Emblemata: Handbuch zur Sinnbildkunst des XVI. und XVII. Jahrhunderts* (Stuttgart, 1967), p. 779.

[10] Albrecht Schöne, *Emblematik und Drama im Zeitalter des Barock* (München, 1964), pp. 104-05.

the conclusion, moreover, become counterbalanced, the more strikingly since each clause contains a broken line. Finally, two sentences of virtually identical length flank this core of the sestet and summit of the poem: in one the tension rises, preparatory to a climax; in the other it wanes as the poem reaches its close.

Sonnet 34 is more grandly conceived but less perfectly executed.

34
Auf die GOtt-beliebende Glaubens stärke.

WEil dir der starke Glaub / das Allmacht-Mark aussaugen /
mein Herrscher / so gefiel / daß Mosen du gestrafft /
als zweiflend' er gewankt an jenes Felsen Safft.
    Wird / mein' Erz-zuversicht in deine güt / was taugen.
    Er hat / was hartes zwar / doch gleichwol was / vor Augen.
Ich häng' entgegen ganz an unsichtbarer krafft:
und ist mir (was noch mehr) gar dunkelhafft geschafft /
das ich es mir oft selbst in meinem Sinn ablaugen:
    doch nur aus Gottes forcht / nicht auß unglaubigheit.
Mein höchster Gott / du weist / wie sehr ich dir die Ehre
der Allmacht gieb' / und glaub' ein eussserst hohe sach.
    Es fliegt in dein' allhöch der Glaube nie zu weit.
Dein unerdenklichs Lob durch dieses wunder mehre.
Mein Glaubens-Felse werd' ein klarer freudenbach.

The poem is not a dialectical exercise, but rather a pathetic argument—an argument designed not only to convince, but also to move. Its object is God. It begins in the first strophe with a logical proof and rises thereafter to an appeal. The first three lines are an inverted deduction which constitutes a proposition. From the penalty which God exacted of Moses after the Israelites rebelled for want of water in the desert (Numbers 20, 2-13), the poet deduces that faith, which she equates by apposition with "aussaugen des Allmacht-Marks," is eminently pleasing to God.[11] On the basis of this proposition, she concludes (line 4) that her utter faith in God's goodness will not fail of its effect.

In the second strophe she elaborates. She uses the example of Moses now not as a proposition, but as a foil to her own situation. The contrast enables her to strengthen her argument. The familiar example offers a further advantage. If Moses' experience can be contrasted with the poet's, then their respective situations must be comparable. This implied similarity permits the poet to speak vaguely of her own situation; with reference to Moses, she can express herself clearly without ever being precise. Like him, she is waiting for a miracle; unlike him, she has

---

[11] Her interpretation distorts the sense of the scripture. Moses was punished not because he hesitated to strike water from the rock—he did not hesitate—but because he failed to defend God before his frightened and clamoring people: Numbers 20, 12.

the benefit of no visible sign (such as a rock) that this miracle will be accomplished.

In the middle of the second strophe begins the development which mars the construct of the poem. Line 7 intensifies the statement in line 6. It raises the poet's dependence upon invisible power to a state of general obscurity, and this obscurity in turn leads to the confession in line 8: in her ignorance of God's intentions for her (line 7) the poet often denies "it" in her intellect (= "Sinn"). "Es" in line 8 is an external reference. It is that something to which the poet refers repeatedly in these poems and which she never explains. Doubtless it is the same miracle to which she alludes ever so covertly in the analogy between her situation and Moses' in lines 5-6.

The statement in line 8 is qualified. The inflection of the verb ("laugen" = *leugnen*), while dictated by the rhyme, implies also an elided modal—*will* or *muß*—which diminishes the force of the verb. The denial, moreover, takes place "in meinem Sinn." The polarity of faith and reason is a recurrent theme in the sonnets.[12] Here, then, the denial is qualified so that it might leave the poet's faith, professed in line 4, unimpaired. Nevertheless, line 8 carries the intensification which began in line 5 past the proper point—with respect both to content and to space. The poet finds herself obliged to introduce an explicit limitation which will also round off the strophe. In line 9 she carefully points out that the denial is prompted only by her mindfulness of God ("Gottes forcht"), not by loss of faith. Only in this line does the tone of the delivery fall again. Lines 5-8 have risen steadily, each setting forth a stronger statement than its predecessor. The rhyme scheme, however, and an analogy to the first strophe, which culminates between the *weil*-clause in lines 1-3 and the principal clause in line 4, predispose this passage toward culmination at the end of line 7, the sense of the lines notwithstanding. The extension of the second strophe into line 9 has thrown the poem's first long movement off balance.

It damages the second movement, which begins in line 10, no less seriously. Just as the first strophe is a conventional quatrain, lines 10-12 are a conventional first tercet. The tone rises sharply as the poet renders from her argument also an appeal. In lines 10-11 she insists upon her faith with great urgency, speaking in superlatives and calling God as her witness. "Eir. eussert hohe sach" at the end of line 11 is again an outside reference. Here it defines itself more precisely, for the adjective echoes "mein höchster Gott" in line 10 and "allhöch," God's exaltedness, in line 12. The "sach," then, has godly qualities and is mentioned in the midst of godly qualities. This second reference places this thing the poet desires into the immediate context of her faith just before the poem reaches its pinnacle. Heretofore she has claimed and argued her

---

[12] Sonnet 28, lines 5-7; sonnet 30, lines 9-11; sonnet 48, lines 3 and 8; sonnet 68 passim; sonnet 205, lines 1-8; sonnet 209, lines 13-14.

faith; at the height of the poem in line 12 she enacts it. The statement itself is an act of faith. It is that deed which, according to the definition of faith in line 1, will enlist God's omnipotence, mentioned explicitly again in line 11.

Lines 13-14 lie on a descending plane. The argument, which has been first logical and then more and more urgently insistent, ascending to a dramatization of itself in line 12, drops to a gently phrased petition. "Dieses wunder" in line 13 is probably a third outside reference. Conceivably it may be an anticipation of the appeal advanced in line 14, in which case a colon at the end would punctuate line 13 properly. This reading, however, produces a small logical inconsistency. The miracle which the poet requests would be the transformation of her faith into joy. It is more reasonable, and it enhances the poem, to assume that the miracle she has in mind is something of much greater moment—"ein eusserst hohe sach"—and that the accomplishment of this miracle, as requested in line 13, will produce consequently the change described in line 14. In this case line 14 is not a withheld clarification of "dieses wunder," which would require rising intonation, but a corollary to the fulfillment of the request in line 13. As an attendant phenomenon, it deserves a lighter stress, and this gentler tone is in keeping both with the mode of the optative verb and with the delicacy of the picture.

This final picture in a poem which is almost without metaphors wraps up the piece materially and formally. It ties the ultimate request to the example of Moses, from which the argument and subsequently the petition emanated. In this context it makes the change which it describes also a miracle, a secondary miracle to accompany the greater wonder requested in line 13. That the poet should conceive of the transformation of her faith into joy also as a miracle implies once more the keenness of her longing, the extent to which she is personally committed to the unnamed purpose for which she begs God's intercession. The metaphor is internally fruitful. "Fels" gives "Glaube" the strength and monumental immobility of a cliff, and "bach" makes "freude" clear and pure, lively and bright. The two in combination and with incidental reference to the original example give "Glaube" a concomitant connotation of actual (though not potential) unproductiveness and "freude" water's archetypal qualities of fertility and fruitfulness.

For all this, the conclusion of the poem is flawed because it lacks perfect balance. The ascent through three lines and three rhymes is answered by a descent through two lines. Despite the content, despite the metaphor, the second movement of the poem does not reach full rhythmic repose. The resolution seems truncated. And yet the very magnitude of this sonnet's intellectual process gives it stature superior to perfectly constructed sonnet 9.

The spectrum of Greiffenberg's methods of composition is an account also of her attempts to gain control of her poems. This account has its vicissitudes. In the linear poems the poet is troubled most seriously by her difficulties with insufficiency. Her method—accumulation of discrete examples—sustains her only from one line to the next. She is driven into an unrelenting search for new material, and this search distracts her from any attempt to consider the arrangement and balance of her presentation. In the poems made up of discrete blocks her control extends to the strophe, and this control becomes more assured according to the various methods of the block poems. In the poems which repeat without predominant pictures the poet is less at the mercy of alien laws than in the repetitive poems whose strophes depend upon a consistent picture.

In all these poems Greiffenberg derives whatever control she exercises from a standardized procedure—linear accumulation or repetition—and the very standardization of these procedures restricts the possibilities of the poems. Yet on the balance, the standard methods help the poems more than they damage them, for when Greiffenberg forgoes the methods, she loses all control and produces in the largest single group of poems by any procedure—the amassed sonnets—the most disorderly pieces in the collection. Then the balance tips. Even in the absence of a standard method, the poet is able to compose consistent strophes of clear and reasonable relevance to one another. She gains sovereign command of her composition. She practices this command on a modest scale, restricting herself to certain clear arrangements of her discourse—intensification of the expression, enlarged setting for a poem's idea—and then on a grand scale. These are the fully integrated sonnets.

Within these poems, too, the poet's control varies. In a few pieces which I have placed at the beginning of the group she depends upon schematic outlines. Without these schemes, she controls first only the two quatrains. Then she comes into command of the full sonnet and exercises this command more and more vigorously. She mobilizes the material, the idea, and finally—in the fully integrated exclamation and argument—the very form of the sonnet in the service of one another and of the larger whole these three then constitute.

CHAPTER SEVEN

GREIFFENBERG AND GRYPHIUS

Greiffenberg's perennial difficulty is meagerness. Throughout the collection she suffers from ideas which fail to develop and consequently from a paucity of germane material in which to present these static ideas. Her response is to force material into an inchoate poem, either by means of a standard method of composition or—in the absence of such a method—with undisciplined abandon. These compensatory measures play such a large role in Greiffenberg's production that they tend to gain control of her poems and to govern them by laws indigenous not to the potential logic of a piece, but to the method by which it is composed. The collection is a record of the poet's attempts to discipline the vagaries of autonomous method. The consequence of these attempts is a broad and intricate scale of quality. The study of Greiffenberg's poems becomes a pathology of the sonnet.

Gryphius' poems present an entirely different picture. The one hundred sonnets in his first two books[1] reflect the same broad types of organization which are to be found in Greiffenberg's collection: there are linear pieces, poems made up of discrete blocks, and integrated sonnets. But the distribution of the poems within these groups and the methodological development from one group to another reveal a poet of another order, with his own strengths and liabilities and his own methods of taking these into account.

Gryphius' linear poems are few: four in the collection of one hundred. Of these only one (book II, sonnet VII) is an example of Greiffenberg's stratagem of accumulating new material in the form of one-line aphorisms. Another (II/IX) is a deliberate exercise in stichomythia—a dubious enterprise for a sonnet, in which the relationship of the strophes to one another is of capital importance. Two of these poems however (I/XLIV and II/XL) are deliberate and reasonably successful exploitations of linear delivery.

The repetitive sonnets are Gryphius' second largest group. Here, too, he largely refrains from using his method of delivery to introduce new material into a faltering poem. Only in sonnets I/IV and I/XLIX is

---

[1] The text is that of the 1663 edition, the *Ausgabe letzter Hand;* see above, p. 56 n. 1. For the purposes of this comparison, I have ignored Books III and IV, the *Sonn- und Feiertagssonette*. The constraints of periphrase make these poems unsuitable for comparison with Greiffenberg's largely free compositions.

repetition obviously a means of filling blank space. Elsewhere the poet is preoccupied with developing his available resources. His progress in the repetitive sonnets appears in an increasing sovereignty over his material, a more sure-handed exploitation of its intellectual and rhetorical possibilities, until he produces three sonnets (I/XI, II/X, II/XXXIX) whose excellence derives from their very repetitiveness.

The amassed sonnets are the largest group in Greiffenberg's collection. In Gryphius' work they are the second smallest. Amassment, moreover, is a misnomer here. Characteristically Greiffenberg's amassed poems are of strikingly disparate content, reflecting an uncontrolled grasping for new material. The content of Gryphius' corresponding pieces is more consonant. He appears not to have sought frantically for new material but rather to have deposited his available supplies in a heap. The sonnets are more accurately described as unassimilated. The poet's task is to sort his material, to gather it into harmonious groups, and to develop its content.

In this distinction between Greiffenberg's amassed sonnets and Gryphius' unassimilated pieces lies the fundamental difference between their creative procedures. The two poets approach the sonnet from opposite directions. Greiffenberg is plagued by paucity of material and idea. Her methods of composition are means of accumulating material. Gryphius, as his unassimilated sonnets testify, disposes over a wealth of relevant material. His task is to reduce this material—to shape it formally and to point it up intellectually. Therefore he is one step ahead of Greiffenberg at the outset. He can begin immediately to arrange and refine his pieces. He enjoys a further advantage: since he does not depend upon a standard method for the generation of a sonnet, such a method never comes to tyrannize the poem—or the poet. Gryphius exercises a greater control over his work. This sure management is confirmed in the integrated sonnets, his largest single group of poems. But his starting point is the unassimilated sonnet.

Significantly, among these unassimilated pieces the poems of pure encomium are prominent: the three dedicated to the poet's brother Paul (I/XII, I/XV, I/L), the one on Schönborn's library (I/XIV), and the parting panegyric to Rome (II/XLI). It is as if the poet's enthusiasm for his subject had furnished him with a superabundance of material which for reasons of piety he hesitated to cull and reduce. Sonnets I/XV on Paul Gryphius' exile and I/L on his grave are sufficiently similar in content to demonstrate the poet's progress in the unassimilated poems. The former is the more primitive.

I/XV
PAULI GRYPHII, PHILOSOPHI & Theologi Fratris dulciss. Exilium.

DEr Eyfers voll von Gott hat Tag und Nacht gelehret /
Den Christus Lib entzünd't; den Gottes Geist gerührt /

Der Christus Schafe stets auff grüne Weide führt /
Dem offt die Angst das Hertz / und Glutt das Gut versehret /
Der keiner Feinde Glimpff / noch Schnauben je gehöret /
   Den Tugend hat durch Pein / wie Gold durch Glutt gezihrt /
Der einig nur gelebt als seiner Lehr gebührt /
Den Weißheit ihr erlist / den Svada hoch verehret /
Den hat der Feinde Grimm ins Elend hin verjagt!
   Ins Elend? ey nicht so. Wann diser nach uns fragt /
Der das gewölbte Rund der Erden auffgebauet;
   So mangelt nirgend Platz / der dem diß Hauß zu klein /
   Das Vih und Menschen trägt / zeucht in den Himmel ein /
Der uns zum Vaterland und Wohnung anvertrauet.

The poem divides at line 9. The first section—which the rhyme scheme, reinforced by the conventional practice of the sonnet, breaks at line 4—is a single sentence. It consists of a series of modifiers in the form of relative clauses and a principal clause in line 9, which extends the second strophe beyond the traditional four lines. The second section is precariously attached to the first. The link between "Elend" in line 9 and its echo in line 10 overlooks the import of the relative clauses in lines 1-8. Thus the connection between the two parts of the poem hangs upon a single word. Lines 10-14 proceed to dispute the validity of "Elend." The dispute rises in line 12.1 to an assertion, which lines 12.2-14 explain and prove, so that the second part of the poem breaks into two subsections of two and one-half lines each. The principle underlying the composition of this second section is familiar: the poet challenges his own statement and proves it false. Lines 10-14 are a schematic argument.[2]

The format of the entire poem and particularly of its first section would seem also to be familiar. Lines 1-9 are a single sentence expanded by multiple modifiers of a single direct object. These multiple modifiers are syntactically parallel—all are relative clauses—and with one exception each occupies one line. At the conclusion of this first sentence the poem breaks distinctly. The organization of the poem resembles that of Greiffenberg's syntactically subordinate list. A comparison of Gryphius' poem with Greiffenberg's sonnet 65, however, shows that the two poems differ.

The multiple subjects of Greiffenberg's poem are all examples. These examples represent a single unchanging moral principle: constancy toward God. Only insofar as they represent this principle are they germane. Their specific material is diverse and of little consequence. In a word, these multiple subjects are illustrative not informative. Their number could be greatly reduced without diminishing significantly the content of the poem's first sentence. Such is not the case with Gryphius' piece. The multiple modifiers of his sentence record a catalogue of

---

[2] See above, pp. 72-73.

qualities which are germane. They convey relevant information about the poet's brother, who is the subject of the poem, or at least of its first part. Because the specific material of these multiple modifiers conveys relevant information, the series of relative clauses is not intellectually static. Each new clause increases the reader's knowledge of the subject at hand, though the information is of uneven quality and appears in random sequence. Gryphius' extended sentence, then, is not a list. The poet has not introduced a number of examples of indifferent content to represent some static principle or finished idea.

A glance suffices to show that Gryphius' poem is even more remote from Greiffenberg's amassed sonnets. Just as the material of the relative clauses is all germane to the subject of the poem, it is also internally consistent. The poem does not leap from one topic to another as if the poet were grasping after new material; it does not drift aimlessly as if he had permitted the thought to grow at will. The piece offers no evidence that the poet was intent upon augmenting his incipient poem either by accumulating one-line examples or by introducing new material massively. In fact it gives no evidence that the poet was intent upon augmentation at all. Rather he appears simply to have unloaded here the resources which were readily available to him. These readily available resources suffice to fill the necessary space.

The poem has three weaknesses, which can be traced to a common source. The poet has failed to arrange his abundant material logically. His delivery is therefore disorderly, and not only disorderly, but also redundant. Line 3 circumscribes Paul Gryphius' profession (he was a pastor) and reduplicates the more precise description in line 1. Line 6 speaks not only of Paul's virtue, but also of his biographical hardships, and reproduces the information in line 4. Lines 1 and 3, then, speak of Paul's calling; lines 2 and 8 of his gifts; lines 4 and 6 are biographical; and lines 5, 6, 7, and, obliquely, line 1 describe his virtue. The final consequence of the disarray in the poem's material is the most serious of the three. Because the poet has neglected to introduce logical order into his material, he is unable to develop its inherent logic and enlarge upon his topic. Consequently, he is obliged to seek a new departure in line 10.

All three of these failings—disorder, redundancy, and premature exhaustion—are remedied in sonnet I/L on Paul's grave.

I/L
Uber seines Herrn Bruder P. GRYPHII Grab.

HIr ruht / dem keine Ruh' auff diser Welt bescheret:
  Hir ligt der keinmal fil / hir schläfft das hohe Haupt /
  Das für die Kirche wacht / hir ist den GOtt geraubt /
Der voll von GOtt / doch nichts denn GOtt allein begehret.
Der Mañ den GOtt als Gold dreymal durch Glutt bewehret

> Durch Elend / Schwerdt / und Pest / der unverzagt geglaubt:
> Dem Gott nach stetter Angst / hat stete Lust erlaubt
> Nach dem ihn Seuch / und Angst / und Tod umsonst beschweret.
> Dein Bischoff / Crossen! ach! den GOttes Geist entzünd't.
> Dem an Verstand und Kunst man wenig gleiche find't.
> Und des Beredsamkeit kaum einer wird erreichen.
> In dem die Tugend lebt / durch den die Tugend lehrt /
> Mit dem die Tugend starb / dem JEsus itzt verehrt.
> Was sich mit keinem Schatz der Erden läst vergleichen.

The most striking difference between this sonnet and the one above is that here the discourse is continuous. There is no counterpart to the new departure in line 10 of sonnet I/XV. This is not because the poet has produced new material on Paul. The two poems almost reduplicate one another. Rather, the information on Paul suffices to fill fourteen lines here because the poet has developed and exploited the same material he used in the poem on Paul's exile. He is able to develop the material because he has sorted it into logical groups. The first quatrain speaks primarily of Paul's virtue and in overtones of other things, which it brings together by means of an ingenious device. The second quatrain offers biographical information. Paul's gifts appear in the first tercet. In the second tercet his virtue returns in a final panegyric which crowns the piece.

The process by which the poet has developed this carefully sorted material is especially clear in the second quatrain. Line 5—"Der Mann den Gott als Gold dreymal durch Glutt bewehret"—corresponds to line 6 in sonnet I/XV—"Den Tugend hat durch Pein / wie Gold durch Glutt gezihrt." The position of the two lines is germane. In sonnet I/XV the line stands within the second strophe. It is flanked by lines on Paul's virtue. Therefore its biographical implications remain marginal. It refers both to Paul's virtue and to his biography; in both instances the reference is vague. In sonnet I/L the line stands at the beginning of the second quatrain, where it functions as a topic sentence. Using "dreymal" as his hinge, the poet attaches line 6 to the topic broached in line 5 and elaborates: "Elend / Schwerdt / und Pest" enumerate the three instances specifically. The second halfline of 6 is still relevant. Paul's courageous faith substantiates the "Bewährung" asserted in line 5. Line 7 submits divine recognition that Paul has withstood the test: God rewards him. In line 8 the development of the topic founders. The poet becomes redundant. He substitutes "Seuch / und Angst / und Tod" for "Elend / Schwerdt / und Pest" above. "Angst" here repeats the same word in line 7 to no good purpose and violates good diction. "Umsonst," crucial to the sense of line 8, is gratuitous after the information in lines 5-7. Nevertheless Gryphius has converted what was one line in sonnet I/XV into three sound verses here.

In the first tercet the material is developed more modestly. Pallid line 8 of the sonnet on Paul's exile—"Den Weißheit ihr erlist / den Svada hoch verehret"—becomes trenchant and grows to fill lines 10-11. The effect is enhanced because line 2 of sonnet I/XV has been purged of its redundancy, reduced to a halfline, and placed in line 9.2 among other remarks on Paul's gifts.

In the first and last strophes of this sonnet the refinement of the material is more subtle and more crafty. The ingenious device of the first quatrain is paradox. Three times the poet plots a verb of repose against an antonym. These verbs are a continuous thread. They connect the first two and one-half lines of the poem and attach these lines to the title, to Paul's grave. The point of departure, then, is the grave. The thrust of this topic is maintained by the verbs of repose. These verbs, moreover, are linked by paradoxness to their antonyms. This connection draws the second members of the paradoxes into the established stream of discourse and incorporates a variety of information. Without changing the focus of the reader's attention, the poet can say (line 1) that Paul found no peace in this world—which is as much as to say both that he worked tirelessly and that he was persecuted—that he was upright (line 2.1 and 2.2), and that he was a man of God, both as a pastor and privately (lines 2.2-3.1).

In the middle of line 3 the device expires. Here, as in line 8, the quality of the discourse deteriorates. The second halfline of 3 is extraneous to the previous discussion. Its only link to lines 1-3.1 is oblique: in "rauben" (= to abduct) there is an overtone of mourning which is not incompatible with the meditation upon a gravesite implicit in "hir ruht . . . hir ligt . . . hir schläfft." Line 3.2 and line 4 are linked rhetorically: a common field of connotation connects "rauben" and "begehren." The figure is less than entirely successful. "Voll" in line 4.1 is related to "begehren" but not to "rauben." Thus the association of "rauben" and "begehren" leaves line 4.1 imperfectly assimilated. The paradox in line 4, moreover, is largely self-serving. It does not increase the information on Paul available in lines 2-3.1.

The second tercet generalizes the specific information in lines 5 and 7 of sonnet I/XV and combines it under the topic "Tugend." The threefold recurrence of "Tugend" and the parallelism of the prepositional constructions in lines 12-13.1 draw the verbs "leben . . . lehren . . . sterben" into a continuum. The logic of these verbs describes a biography of virtue which parallels Paul's career and transforms him into an apotheosis of virtue. Fittingly, the second tercet becomes a synoptic eulogy, exceeding the praise in the rest of the sonnet. The rhythm reinforces the sense of the lines. The parallel constructions break the passage into halflines, so that the pace of the delivery accelerates. The distinctions among the prepositions "in . . . durch . . . mit" entail a contrastive intonation which becomes pointed over the third member of the series. The initial foot of line 13 is reversed. "Mit" carries the first stress, and this sudden emphasis throws a bright light upon the drastic statement at the climax of the sequence. Line 13.2

follows from the rest and functions as a denouement. The last line gathers up the whole passage and yields a final judgment on the value of the things described here.

A combination of good rhetoric and solid substance has changed the raw material of lines 1-3.1 and of the last tercet into fine poetry. In the first quatrain synonymous verbs and their paradoxes incorporate a quantity of relevant information into a stream of discourse which proceeds from the title of the poem. In the second tercet parallelism draws together three verbs whose logic transforms the subject of the poem, making Paul a supreme representative of virtue. In both passages the rhetoric serves to make the material fruitful and graceful. The criteria then are that the material be substantial and the rhetoric functional. Rhetoric alone, be it ever so orderly, will not refine a crude poem. In sonnet II/XLVII Gryphius presses rhetorical assimilation beyond its functional possibilities.

II/XLVII
Das Letzte Gerichte.

AUff Todten! auff! die Welt verkracht in letztem Brande!
  Der Sternen Heer vergeht! der Mond ist dunckel-rott /
  Die Sonn' ohn allen Schein! Auff / ihr die Grab und Kott
Auff! ihr die Erd und See und Hellen hilt zu Pfande!
Ihr die ihr lebt komm't an: der HErr / der vor in Schande
  Sich richten liß / erscheint / vor Ihm laufft Flam̃' und Noth
  Bey Ihm steht Majestätt / nach ihm / folgt Blitz und Tod /
Umb ihn / mehr Cherubim als Sand an Pontus Strande.
Wie liblich spricht Er an / die seine Recht' erkohren.
  Wie schrecklich donnert Er / auff dise / die verlohren.
  Unwiderrufflich Wort / kommt Freunde / Feinde flíht!
Der Himmel schleust sich auff! O GOtt! welch frölich scheiden;
  Die Erden reist entzwey. Welch Weh / welch schrecklich Leiden.
  Weh / Weh dem / der verdam't: wol dem / der JEsum siht!

The material of the poem is grouped with stringent orderliness, and these groups follow logically. In the first quatrain the dead are summoned as the universe disintegrates. In the second quatrain, after a halfline summons to the living which disturbs the strict order and produces a slight logical discrepancy, the Lord appears in judgment. In the first tercet he sits in judgment. In the second tercet his judgment is executed. In each instance the pertinent material suffices to fill a strophe.

For all its orderliness, logic, and sufficiency of germane material, however, the sonnet rings hollow. The fault lies equally in the content of the piece and in its rhetoric, and the weakness becomes more pronounced as the poem progresses. The first strophe, while by no means great, is acceptable enough. The poet integrates a description of the destruction at Doomsday into his threefold summons to the dead with fair skill. He enlarges both the summons and the description by means of syntactical parallels, using in each instance a series of words which share a common realm and thus suggest one another: "Welt . . . Sterne . . . Mond . . . Sonn'" in the description, "Grab . . . Kott . . . Erd . . . See . . . Helle" (= *Hölle*) in the summons. The redundancy in "Grab . . . Kott . . . Erd" is not serious and is partially compensated insofar as the very enumeration of these heightens the solemnity of the summons. The same may be said of the description. The details of what is happening to the world, the stars, the moon, and the sun are of little value in their own right, but the express mention of each of these lends a quality of awesomeness to the destruction. The poet achieves a rhetorical effect at the cost of a certain insubstantiality of content.

The first quatrain is no worse than mediocre. Its mediocrity, however, damages the second quatrain seriously. The strophe begins badly. The extension of the summons beyond its proper preserve in lines 1-4 and the logical weakness of attaching lines 5.2-8 more directly to the summons to the living than to the summons to the dead are minor offenses. More injurious is the extended figure of thought. The principle basic to the composition of the first quatrain is proliferation of words: "Welt" in line 1 suggests "Sterne . . . Mond . . . Sonn'" in lines 2-3.1. "Grab und Kott" in line 3 suggests "Erd . . . See . . . Helle" in line 4. This same proliferation persists in the second quatrain, where "Ihr die ihr lebt" in line 5 responds to "Auff Todten!" in line 1. The logic is unexceptionable. The offense lies in the rhetorical device, which begins here to sacrifice the modest merits of its effect to the tedium of its omnipresence.

In lines 6.2-8 the tedium increases to the point of obscuring content. The proliferation of words, introduced into the second quatrain by the echo of "leben" in line 5 to "tot" in line 1, begins again in earnest with the series of prepositions "vor . . . bey . . . nach . . . umb." The effect of continuing sameness is heightened by the syntactical parallelism and by the steady rhythm of breaks at the halfline, both of which repeat the practice of lines 2-3.1. The implication is that the poet has fastened upon a convenient mechanism and is composing automatically. The implication is false, for the content of lines 6.2-7 is rich. "Flamm' und Noth" which precede the Lord are the destruction and misery of Doomsday; the majesty which accompanies him is the emblem of his office, the sign of his assumption into heaven, and the word contrasts pointedly with "Schande" in line 5; "Blitz und Tod" which follow him represent the damnation which will ensue upon his judgment. These levels of meaning are obscured behind the wearisome enumeration of prepositions, which, moreover, places all the points of description on a plane with line 8, where a wider referent is missing.

In the first tercet the sonnet does indeed degenerate into automatic composition. Line 9 plots "lieblich" against "schrecklich" in line 10.

Parallel syntax of the two lines follows perforce. In the ludicrously alliterative and vacuous plotting of pairs "Freunde / Feinde fliht" at the end of line 11 the sonnet reaches its low point. The second tercet continues to weigh the saved against the damned; the parallelism persists; the content of the opposite qualities becomes more and more impoverished. The poem has become predictable.

In these three sonnets Gryphius has run the gamut from unassimilated amorphousness to hyper-assimilated rigidity. He has refined his poems by gathering their material into consonant groups, elaborating the content, and assimilating, primarily by means of rhetorical devices. In the third poem he reaches and exceeds the limits of rhetorical assimilation. The enterprise has not been very profitable. It yields in the last analysis orderly poems with occasional fine passages when there is a particularly happy conjunction of rhetoric and material. Yet Gryphius acquits himself better than Greiffenberg. He retains a free hand over his material, while she forfeits her control to promiscuous amassment. He is able to organize and arrange while she leaps from topic to topic. While she tries to correct flagrant offenses—disjunctiveness, hypertrophied passages, diverted discourse—he can look at leisure for a means of making his material fruitful. He has not a few talents which help him in this search. Quite aside from the abundance of relevant material at his disposal, Gryphius has a keen sense for the logic of his material—for what belongs together, for the sequence of these groups. He is aware of the effects of his delivery. His rhythms are elastic, and at their best—as in the final tercet of sonnet I/L—they are purposefully varied. The transgressions in sonnet II/XLVII notwithstanding, he has an adept hand at rhetoric. His task now is to use these abilities not only to organize his material, but also to exploit it: to develop its intellectual potential and its connotative possibilities.

The first step toward deepening the sonnets is simple and obvious: the poet narrows his topic. He gives up broad eulogies and descriptions and defines his subject precisely. In these poems the theme for which he is famous—vanitas mundi—becomes prominent. The format of the sonnet is also simple. Gryphius uses repetitive delivery, but the nature and the purpose of his repetitiveness differs from Greiffenberg's.

The crudest of these repetitive poems with narrow focus, I/XLVIII "An sich selbst," lapses into the disorder characteristic of the unassimilated sonnet on Paul's exile. Even a cursory comparison with two other sonnets of very similar subject matter, I/IX and I/XLV both entitled "Thränen in schwerer Kranckheit," suffices to show that here the poet has dismembered his body at random. He flits from symptom to symptom, describes his complaints vaguely, juxtaposes them arbitrarily, and neglects their larger implication until the second tercet. Here he plunges abruptly into the meaning of all this and achieves his sole moment of high pathos in line 14.

The disorder and vagueness of this poem cannot be corrected merely by gathering the material into consonant groups. The subject of the sonnet is so narrow that all the material belongs within substantially the same group. It does not lend itself to fine differentiation. Such essential sameness would be no blemish if the idea inherent in the material were sufficiently developed to admit distinctions. The poem is superficial. It lacks intellectual thrust.

A sustaining idea and the beginnings of deliberate form appear in sonnet I/XX:

I/XX
Grabschrifft eines trefflichen Vorsprechers.

ICh / der durch alle Netz die ernsten Rechte brach /
Dem an Verstand und Kunst kaum imand gleich zu schätzen
Der sich für keinem Thron noch Richtstul kont entsetzen
Verlohr / als mir der Tod mein endlich Urtheil sprach.
Der wolberedte Mund / der gleich der stoltzen Bach
Sich unverzagt ergoß / der ide zu verletzen
Und trösten mächtig war / vergaß sein weises Schwätzen /
Der strenge Richter gab mir keine Frist mehr nach.
Er schloß die Augen zu / dem nichts verschlossen war!
Der Kärcker brach und schloß / den schleust die enge Bahr:
Was hilfft mich / daß ich vor befördert so vil Sachen?
Das mich mein Gegentheil offt mit Entsetzen hört
Das wer mich recht erkänt / mich mit Bestürtzung ehrt?
Nun nichts mich von dem Spruch des Todes loß kan machen.

The organization of the poem is modest, clear, and carefully controlled. It resembles that of Greiffenberg's repetitive sonnets with compound basic thought (see above, pp. 51-54). Both facets of the compound appear in the first quatrain. In lines 1-3 the speaker delivers in a broad and general description a thumbnail sketch of himself. Line 4, which resolves the relative clauses of the description, strikes the tonic note of the poem: death nullifies all human qualities, all human endeavor. The metaphor reinforces the sense of the statement. The speaker was a barrister. In line 3 he refers specifically to his boldness before the court. In line 4, however, death takes charge of the courtroom: death delivers the final verdict, and this verdict is against the barrister ("*mein endlich Urtheil*"). This subtle touch moves the barrister into a dual role. He becomes both the advocate and the accused before the court, and it is a case against himself which he loses. Thus death defeats him precisely in that capacity which he cites in lines 1-3 as his characteristic quality. The first quatrain is not purely descriptive. The statement in line 4 interprets and enriches the implications of the material in lines 1-3.

The second quatrain repeats the first with purposeful variation. Lines 5-7.1 follow up the broad characterization in lines 1-3 with detail. Appropriately, the passage focuses on the advocate's mouth, the proper organ of his profession. Line 7.2 renders the statement in line 4 in terms consistent with the new focus. Once again the advocate has been undone at the center of his person. Line 8 recasts line 7.2 and reverts to the original conceit of death as a judge. This double conclusion to the quatrain produces more than metaphoric consistency. It changes the texture of the delivery. The first quatrain is dense. The subject at the beginning of line 1 is separated from its predicate in line 4 by three relative clauses. Because they retard the completion of the sentence, these clauses make the syntax turgid. The effect is only heightened at the moment of release, for the verb which unlocks the sense of all three lines is simple and intransitive—a single word. Abruptly the sense and the syntax of the sentence are completely resolved. The second quatrain is perceptibly less tense. Only two relative clauses stand between the subject in line 5.1 and the predicate in line 7.2. The clauses themselves are not as rigorous as those above. The first is expanded by a nonessential adverbial modifier; the verb of the second comprises two complementary infinitives. The arrangement of these clauses so that they bridge the ends of lines 5 and 6 and meet at midline in 6 promotes their fluidity. More pertinently, here the space occupied by the relative clauses contrasts less starkly with that required by the subject and the verb of the principal clause. The subject of the main clause is enlarged to include a noun and two modifiers, and the transitive verb requires completion in a direct object, again with modifiers. Finally, the subject and the relative clauses are resolved gently. The resolution extends through the recasting of line 7.2 in line 8. This slackening continues throughout the rest of the poem.

Lines 9 and 10 belong together and constitute a strophe. They are rhymed as a couplet; the chiastic position of their respective principal and relative clauses makes one line the mirror image of the other. For all their succinctness, however, the two lines are closely related to line 8, which they elaborate. Thus the first facet of the poem's thought, the characteristics of the speaker, is developed in lines 5-7 and the second, the power of death over the speaker, in lines 8-10. The very succinctness of lines 9-10, their jingle-like quality, works like a closing to the piece. They bring a long passage to a halt.

The poet rectifies this premature finale adroitly. The concluding movement, lines 11-14, recapitulates the opening strophe. It takes up once again the broad, general description of the advocate, but this time with a difference. The retardation and turgidity in lines 1-4 is replaced by instant lucidity of sense and syntax. "Was hilfft mich" at the beginning of line 11 clarifies the import of lines 11-13 at the outset. There follows a series of simple *daß*-constructions. Line 14 brings the expected conclusion. "Spruch" here responds to "Urtheil" in line 4 and reconfirms the original metaphor.

The poem is tidily organized. The two facets of its thought appear in the first quatrain. The midsection, which the close attachment between lines 9-10 and line 8 extends across six verses, elaborates each of these facets in turn. A final quatrain recapitulates and confirms the opening movement. The sonnet is frankly and gracefully repetitive. It is, however, of no great stature. Its intellectual dimensions, though more finely differentiated and more highly developed than those of sonnet I/XLVIII, are small. A single compound thought is manipulated skillfully, so that it fills fourteen lines. The thought is already complete in the first quatrain. Mere variations follow. No new dimensions open in the course of the poem. The connotative qualities and metaphoric possibilities of the language are but meagerly exploited. The metaphor of death as the judge before whom the advocate stands is maintained with expert consistency, but after its initial appearance in line 4 it gains no new powers of meaning. Finally the structure of the poem, its repetitiveness, serves no essential function in the presentation of the idea. It merely enables the poet to spread a small thought over a fairly large space. To his credit, he is able both to stretch his thought and to maintain the equipoise of his sonnet.

In sonnet I/XI, the justly celebrated "Menschliches Elende," Gryphius surmounts all these difficulties. The poem is a superb example of perfectly functional repetitiveness.

I/XI
Menschliches Elende.

WAs sind wir Menschen doch? ein Wohnhauß grimmer Schmertzen
   Ein Ball des falschen Glücks / ein Irrlicht diser Zeit.
   Ein Schauplatz herber Angst / besetzt mit scharffem Leid /
Ein bald verschmeltzter Schnee und abgebrante Kertzen.
   Diß Leben fleucht davon wie ein Geschwätz und Schertzen.
   Die vor uns abgelegt des schwachen Leibes Kleid
   Und in das Todten-Buch der grossen Sterblikeit
Längst eingeschriben sind / sind uns aus Sinn und Hertzen.
   Gleich wie ein eitel Traum leicht aus der Acht hinfällt /
   Und wie ein Strom verscheust / den keine Macht auffhält:
So muß auch unser Nahm / Lob / Ehr und Ruhm verschwinden /
   Was itzund Athem holt / muß mit der Lufft entflihn /
   Was nach uns kommen wird / wird uns ins Grab nachzihn
Was sag ich? wir vergehn wie Rauch von starcken Winden.

The sonnet assaults its subject, human misery or more accurately the misery of human transience, four times—once in each of its perfectly regular strophes. Each assault is different. Each develops new ramifications of its topic, so that the thought develops continuously. Each opens new fields of connotative significance, demonstrating in a steadily growing proof the universality of the thought. Each contributes in turn to a consistent and sustained rhetorical effect whose ultimate achievement is sublime pathos.

The sonnet opens abruptly. The rhetorical question elicits five responses which all circumscribe the same thought—the misery of human existence—while no two cover the same ground. The variety lies in their wealth of connotation and in the rhythm of their syntax. The responses in line 1.2 and line 3 have much in common. Both describe man as a scene or setting in which pain resides. Thus they attribute a radical passivity to man: he does not even suffer; rather suffering inhabits him, occupies him as a cast of actors occupies a stage. There is a difference, however, between a dwelling place ("Wohnhauß": line 1) and a stage or arena ("Schauplatz": line 3). The former has a permanence which the latter lacks. And indeed transience is that aspect of human misery which emerges in the course of the five responses to the initial question. The first response connotes passivity and intense pain; the second raises the passivity to the point of making man the object, the toy, of arbitrary forces. This particular toy is a ball, so that motion, which is inextricably bound up in time, is introduced into the series of definitions. In the third response the connotation of motion becomes explicit, for the fundamental characteristic of the will o' the wisp is its elusiveness—it flickers first here, then there. This elusiveness comprehends also an implication of aimlessness, of senseless wandering, more readily accessible in the German "*Irr*licht" than in its English equivalent. And elusiveness is inconstancy of being: just as a swamp light vanishes suddenly and mysteriously, human life too is subject to abrupt and inexplicable extinction. The correlation between light and life is obvious.

Transitoriness has appeared in the series. It is preserved in the fourth response, for the actors who give life to a stage and the play upon a stage are passing phenomena. Here sound as an event in time suggests itself gently. It is held in abeyance until the second quatrain. Line 4 brings two definitions which are a single response. Transience is now overt, for the melted snow and the exhausted candle are emblematic representations of mortality.[3] Transitoriness remains the principal factor of human misery throughout the rest of the poem.

The rhythm of the delivery has become more fluent in each of the first four lines. In line 1 the caesura falls between the opening question and the beginning of the reply, precipitating a weighty pause. The break at midline is less exaggerated but still distinct in line 2, where it divides the second and third responses. In line 3 it becomes gentle, merely subdividing a single definition. It is absorbed in line 4 into the continuous flow of the final rejoinder.

---

[3] Dietrich Walter Jöns, *Das "Sinnen-Bild": Studien zur allegorischen Bildlichkeit bei Andreas Gryphius* (Stuttgart, 1966), pp. 246, 254.

Line 5 begins a second assault. The line is a topic sentence; the rest of the quatrain follows from it. Here sound as an event in time, suggested only marginally in line 3, becomes explicit. Its power to signify transitoriness is reinforced by the nature of this sound: "Geschwätz und Schertzen." These are trivial conversations, those which are quickly forgotten. The quality of triviality carries over also to life, to which the conversations are compared. Line 6 introduces the specific aspect of the subject which this strophe examines: the transitoriness of our ancestors. The metaphor is double: genitive identification ("des schwachen Leibes Kleid") changes the body into a garment; to cast off this garment is to die. The figure recalls the theater in line 3 and in this conjunction it evokes the ephemerality of the dramatic personage, who vanishes when the actor discards his costume. The sentence continues into line 7 and runs without pause to the end of the relative clause at midline in 8. A new metaphor for death appears: to die is to be recorded in the book of the dead, the record of mortality. An old notion, that of the permanence of the written record, of the immortality of books, is being reversed here. The inversion is complete in line 8.2, where it is finished with a cruel touch: our predecessors, who have vanished like characters from a stage, who have been entered into the record of mortality, have disappeared not only from our memory but also from our affections ("aus Sinn und Hertzen"). The delivery has continued to gain fluency. The topic sentence in line 5 is followed by a single sentence which flows continuously to the abutment of the relative clause with the principal clause in the middle of line 8. By virtue of the relative clause, the sentence is syntactically complex and highly integrated.

In the first tercet the third assault on the subject turns from our ancestors to ourselves. Metaphors, which mesh their proper and their metaphoric terms to the point of transforming the referents, yield to simile, which juxtaposes its members while preserving the integrity of each. The comparison to a dream in line 9 is a traditional figure which retains its validity even in the modern language. Not only does it rest upon the dream's peculiar capacity to be forgotten; it evokes also the irreality of the dream, its diaphonous quality. The stream in line 10 is also ancient, having its classic representation in the teachings of Heraclitus. Like the will o' the wisp in line 2, it is another and a more pure example of motion in time. The stream is the flux of human affairs, their inconstancy, their inexorable passing. The opposite member of the comparison appears in line 11. The delay has lent it weight. The four terms of which it is composed contribute again to its prominence. These terms are carefully ordered. The vowels alternate between the middle range and the dark sounds. The words appear in ascending succession, citing more and more powerful manifestations of possible mundane immortality. The ascent elevates this member of the comparison once more. These elaborate preparations sharpen the efficacy of "verschwinden": one word wipes out the entire passage.

The syntax has undergone an interesting change. The second quatrain consists of a topic sentence and another three-line sentence of complex and carefully integrated syntactical structure. In the first tercet a topic sentence is missing. No stable archway stands over the opening of the strophe. The design of the stanza is becoming atectonic. The main body of the discourse, which begins immediately, consists of a complex sentence. This sentence, however, is not as finely integrated as the one above. There the subject of the main clause appears in line 6 and the sense of the sequence is suspended until the completion of this clause in the second half of line 8. Here each clause is intact and each occupies a single line. The compound conjunction "gleichwie . . . so," moreover, gives all the clauses a semblance of equivalence. In keeping with the mechanics of the simile, the members of the comparison are set forth on the same plane. Thus for all the technical complexity of its syntax, the sentence tends to fall into its constituent elements.

The last tercet takes up the final aspect of transitoriness—the ephemerality of our progeny. In the first tercet, the metaphors of the second quatrain were replaced by simile. Here the simile gives way to simple correspondences between words: "Athem . . . Lufft" in line 12, "nach uns kommen . . . uns . . . nachzihn" in line 13. Like the syntactical organization of the strophes, the imagery is ever more tenuously integrated. The relationship between "Athem" and "Lufft" harbors irony. The two words have a common material referent. Yet one describes the badge of life and the other the evanescence which is death. Death is present in the essence of life. Line 13 moves on to the new aspect of the discussion in this strophe. The link between the verbs, reinforced by the pivot "wird / wird" at midline, describes a see-saw process of continuous replacement by our progeny and subsequent displacement of just this progeny. The hinge "itzund . . . nach" between lines 12 and 13 makes the process perpetual. Here the principle fundamental to the composition of the poem—repetitiveness—gains ultimate sense. Just as death recurs in generation after generation, the sonnet repeats its basic thought—the misery of human mortality—in strophe after strophe. The repetition represents the ineluctability of death. Coupled with a consistent tone of resignation, it suggests man's helplessness in the face of the inevitable.

The rhetorical question in line 14 builds briefly to a gentle climax. The comparison which follows is undistinguished to the point of being commonplace. No grand gesture closes the piece. It ends with another example, of no greater value than the many others, of the pervasiveness of death. The syntactical organization of the strophe has become extremely simple. Each line is a single sentence. Like the transient being described here, the poem's rhetoric and structure give way slowly and decompose.

Greiffenberg uses repetition primarily as a means of introducing new material into a faltering poem. Her tendency is to circumscribe in strophe after strophe one fixed and unchanging thought. Her favored device, repetition involving a series of pictures, leads her into a host of difficulties: either the pictures drive the thought into unexpected turns or the thought coerces and contorts the pictures. Even where pictures play no major role in Greiffenberg's repetitive sonnets, repetition itself performs no essential function. Its purpose is extraneous to the poem. It is a means of compensating the poet's inadequacy. For this reason she is at pains to disguise her method.

Gryphius is untroubled by these difficulties. In his weakest repetitive poems he merely disposes carelessly of an adequate quantity of material on a narrow topic. In his mediocre poems (II/LXVI is an example) he uses repetition to drive home a point for whose disposition he has no other inspiration. In his better pieces he begins to display those poetic capacities which enable him to give repetition a genuine function in his sonnets: he is able to differentiate and to refine his thought, and he is alive to the possibilities of form. Sonnet I/XX is no masterpiece. For all its repetitiveness, however, it does not simply drone forth one fixed and finished idea. The repetition which begins in the second strophe, while it does not enlarge the dimensions of the thought, nevertheless makes a fine distinction. It fastens upon one pertinent detail, the advocate's mouth, and to this extent it changes the focus of the delivery. The repetition does not begin again at the zero-point; it assumes what has been said before. It is true that repetition performs no essential service in the presentation of the idea here. Nevertheless, it has formal merits. Not only does it permit the poet to distribute a small idea over a relatively large space. Also the poet is able to exploit his device, to use it to distribute his thought gracefully. Ultimately, the poet, and not the poet's method, controls the progress of the poem.

Sonnet I/XI "Menschliches Elende" is one of Gryphius' finest sonnets. It testifies his command of method. With keen intelligence he identifies various aspects within a single idea. He arranges these aspects in such a fashion that his presentation of an essentially unchanging thought is sustained, differentiated, and continuously developing. For the purposes of his presentation he brings forth a resourceful and richly suggestive body of appropriate material. He disposes of this material with great care and with perfect control, so that the form of the sonnet reinforces its thought, and the three basic components of the poem—idea, material, and form—merge into an inimitable whole.

Indicative of Gryphius' powers as a sonneteer is the large proportion of integrated sonnets he produced. The poems in this final group are not uniformly excellent. But their very number is evidence of the poet's capacity for lo ᠂ ᠂ thought and of his ready command of form. In fact he commands and form with an ease which extends at its lower limit into fac ⋅s. The seven wedding sonnets (I/XXIII, XXV; II/XXI, XXIX X, XXXI, XXXII), all integrated poems, are composed according to a formula. They begin with some description of the external circumstances surrounding the occasion, usually a reference to the season in which the wedding takes place. They incorporate if possible a pun on the couple's name. They go on to extol the conjugal joys which await the pair: love, trust, mutual solace, and of course children. These joys are cast in an allegory proceeding from the pun on the name. Thus Joachim Specht's marriage (sonnet I/XXIII) takes place in the fall. The bridegroom seeks a nest in which he can take refuge from the approaching winter. In the arms of his bride he finds his "Sitz" (= perch = residence: line 12); here many a young "Specht" will be raised (line 14). The poems are trivial to the point of banality. Yet the logic and the order of their presentation are unimpeachable.

In the middle range of Gryphius' integrated sonnets are a number of friendship poems, eulogies, and most of the little noticed satirical pieces. These poems excel in the clear and balanced organization of their statements. They lack the final fusion of thought and material and the august pathos which distinguishes Gryphius' best integrated sonnets. In these all the poet's talents combine: his skills with organization and with rhetoric, with thought, material, and form, as they emerged in the course of the unassimilated and repetitive sonnets, join a capacity for graceful and cogent argument which is typical of integrated sonnets. The result is a fairly large group of exceptionally accomplished poems. Not surprisingly, the theme vanitas mundi comes again to the fore.

The second Eugenie poem (I/XXII) is one of these integrated sonnets. The modifications which Gryphius undertook between the first appearance of the piece in the Lissa collection of 1637[4] and the final version in 1663 reflect the process of purification and arrangement which is typical of his poetic progress.

In the Lissa collection the poem reads:

[XXI]
[An eine hohen Standes Jungfraw.]

Was wundert Ihr Euch noch / Ihr Rose der Jungfrawen /
   Daß diese purpur Roß die Ihr kaum auffgefast
   In Ewr schneeweissen Hand so vnversehns erblast?
So wird Ewr schöner Leib / nach dem Er abgehawen /
   Vons Todes scharffer Seens in kurtzem seyn zu schawen.
   Diß was Ihr jtzt an Euch so lieblich fünckeln last /
   Der Halß / der Mund / die Brust / sol werden so verhast /
Daß jedem / der sie siht / davon wird hefftig grawen.

---

[4] As reproduced in *Andreas Gryphius: Gesamtausgabe der deutschsprachigen Werke,* ed. Marian Szyrocki and Hugh Powell (Tübingen, 1963), vol. I, p. 16. The sonnet is examined in another context by Walter Naumann, *Traum und Tradition in der deutschen Lyrik* (Stuttgart, 1966), pp. 118-24. Fritz Cohen compares the two versions in his article "Two Early Sonnets of Andreas Gryphius: A Study of their Original and Revised Forms," *German Life and Letters,* 25 (1972), 115-26.

> Ewr Seufftzer ist vmbsonst! nichts ist das auff der Welt /
> So schön es jmmer sey Bestand vñ Farbe helt /
> Wir sind von Mutter-Leib zum vntergang erkohren.
> Mag auch an Schönheit was / der Blum zu gleichen seyn?
> Doch / eh sie recht noch blüht verwelckt vnd felt sie ein /
> So greifft der Todt nach vns / so bald wir sind gebohren.

And in the final version:

I/XXII
An Eugenien.

> WAs wundert ihr euch noch / Ihr Rose der Jungfrauen /
> Daß dises Spil der Zeit / die Ros' / in eurer Hand
> Die alle Rosen trotzt / so unversehns verschwand?
> Eugenie so gehts / so schwindet was wir schauen.
> So bald des Todes Senß wird disen Leib abhauen:
> Schau't man den Hals / die Stirn / die Augen / dises Pfand
> Der Libe / dise Brust / in nicht zu rein'sten Sand /
> Und dem / der euch mit Lib itzt ehrt / wird für euch grauen!
> Der Seufftzer ist umbsonst! nichts ist / das auff der Welt /
> Wie schön es immer sey / Bestand und Farbe hält /
> Wir sind von Mutterleib zum Untergang erkohren.
> Mag auch an Schönheit was der Rosen gleiche seyn?
> Doch ehe sie recht blüht verwelckt und fält sie ein!
> Nicht anders gehn wir fort / so bald wir sind geboren.

In both versions the wilting of the rose is an exemplary process from which the poet deduces a larger tendency. In the revised version the deduction is more precise, more cogently argued, and more broadly valid.

The changes in lines 2 and 3 begin straightway to shore up the argument. The two adjectives in the Lissa version, "purpur Roß" and "schneeweisse Hand," are more decorative than functional. They say nothing indispensable about the rose or the hand. Moreover, they are the source of a malfunction. Red is the color of love and of the living, white the color of purity but also of death. The connotations of love and purity are consonant, if superfluous. Those of life and death are troublesome in their attribution here. The poet has placed the rose in the realm of the living and muddied its symbolic appropriateness in this particular poem. He has allied the hand to the realm of the dead, disclosing the girl's mortality before he is ready to argue the point analogically. Finally, "diese purpur Roß . . . erblast" is a sly trick. The personification insinuates into the exemplary process a uniquely human death and arranges for the rose to qualify for its symbolic function here irrespective of its indigenous properties. The deck is stacked.

The emendations purify the symbol, establish its credentials, and straighten out the argument. The reference to redness disappears.

Without prejudicing the case, the appositive in line 2.1 brings forth the flower's chief competent quality. The rose is temporal. The attribute in line 3.1 is no less apposite. The rose is a paragon among roses. Here the correspondence between the girl and the flower becomes twofold. In line 1.2 she is called "Rose der Jungfrauen." On the one hand the epithet states overtly the parallel between the girl and the flower; on the other it turns her into a paragon of womanhood as the blossom is a paragon among roses. A second competence of the rose, its capacity to represent the girl, emerges.

The alteration in line 4 effects a fundamental reorganization of the sonnet. It changes the tone of the entire poem, purges a disingenuous cast to the argument, broadens the applicability of the argument, and prepares for a perfectly controlled reinforcement and extension of the argument in the sestet. In the Lissa version the line marks a new departure in the prosecution of the argument. The poet never justifies the reproach in lines 1-3; he never explains why the girl should not be surprised that the rose has wilted. The analogy which he begins in line 4 cannot function satisfactorily as a justification. She cannot be expected to have observed the parallel between her person and the flower. Inasmuch as she cannot have been aware of this correlation, the poet attacks from ambush. His attack is limited and pointed: it is aimed exclusively at the girl, as if only she were subject to destruction. In the final version the poet is more fair. It is possible that the girl might have observed the ephemerality of the visible world. Thus line 4 justifies the reproach. The tone is gentle: the poet is willing to explain to the girl something she might have seen for herself. And the tone is commiserative: in "wir" the poet includes himself among the bereaved. The explanation enlarges the context of the argument. The poet no longer aims exclusively at the girl's corruptibility, but at a larger phenomenon in which, as he points out in the second quatrain, she too is a participant.

Thus the function of the second strophe changes. Lines 4-8 in the Lissa version are a prolonged attack. Having taken the girl by surprise, the poet slants the analogy to imply that her beauty in particular is susceptible to corruption. Since beauty is probably the most celebrated attribute of the female—her highest attainment according to the myths and the conventions of the civilization—and since beauty (alongside weakness) is a distinguishing characteristic of femaleness—"das schöne Geschlecht"—the poet has directed his attack toward a particularly vulnerable spot. He intensifies his offensive. In line 6 he describes the girl's beauty as an enterprise in which she is personally and willingly engaged. Thus its destruction in line 7 becomes a personal defeat. "Verhast" entails a twofold value judgment, for the resonance of the word embraces both *hassen* and *häßlich*. The antithesis with "lieblich" in line 6 is too obscure and too superfluous to disguise the prejudiced diction. In line 8 the girl is utterly reduced. The verb of the relative clause turns her into a spectacle, or more accurately the verb turns the component parts of her body into a spectacle. She as a human entity has ceased to exist.

The parties to the attack, the focus of the attack, and the ruthlessness of the attack cast an ugly hue over the passage. A man attacks a woman on the subject of her beauty. Obviously he is not a disinterested observer of her mortal susceptibility to death and decay. He has an ax to grind. The analogical demonstration is sullied by an unpleasant air of sexual animosity.

The revision purges this ulterior motive. It also strengthens the logic, clarifies the argument, and brings a number of technical improvements. More consistent logic appears already in the advent of line 4. Not only does the line explain the reproach and broaden the field of the argument. It also enlarges reasonably upon the passing of the rose. The second quatrain follows logically again. The girl's subjection to death and decay is an illustrative example to bear out the general tendency cited in line 4. The poet is still explaining, and for the sake of his point he chooses material which lies close to home. His detachment is evident in his diction in line 5. "Ewr . . . Leib" becomes "diser Leib": he is not interested in the girl's body as such, but only in its pertinence to his point. The adjective vanishes: the body itself, not its beauty, is relevant. The recasting unravels the tangled syntax of lines 4-5 in the Lissa version. The adverbial clause is extracted from its parenthetical position, cast into the active voice, and placed prominently at the beginning of the sentence. In the lucid, active phrasing the metaphoric representation of death as destruction becomes prominent, and a clear parallel between the cutting down of the body and the plucking of the rose emerges. The unfortunate "vons" is corrected and the unnecessary modifier to "Senß" discarded. The introductory clause prepares continuity: the strophe flows with perfect temporal sequence across four lines.

The correction of the tone and the clarification of the idea continue. Line 6 of the original, with its discordant vowels ("Ihr jtzt an Euch") and its pointedly personal reference to the girl, disappears. In its place appears the catalogue of parts of the body, expanded now so that its items gain prominence and moment before they are destroyed abruptly at the end of line 7. The syntax reduplicates the process of destruction and suggests the dimensions of the destruction. The insertion of the appositive "dises Pfand der Libe," which spills over from line 6 into line 7 and thus increases not only the volume but also the fluency and the speed of the series, enriches the sense of the passage. Its conventionally gallant flavor notwithstanding, the phrase endows the catalogue with a cultural reference. It stipulates Eugenie's erotic value and saves the series from simple anatomical enumeration. The stipulation becomes fruitful again in line 8. "Sand" replaces "verhast" at the end of line 7. It is a neutral word, dispassionate and innocent of value judgment. Moreover it is concrete. Its vivid contrast with the delicacy of the girl's body points a third time to the dimensions of the destruction.

Destruction comes to the fore twice in line 8. Here horror proceeds not from the sight of the transformation in various parts of the girl's body—but from the girl herself. Her living person is identified with her corrupted corpse. The revision emends the sweeping "jeder" at the beginning of the line and specifies that the one who honors the girl with love will find her repugnant. Eugenie will lose "Liebe" and "Ehre," which are the manifestations of her primary functions—eros and inspiration—in the long tradition of *Frauenverehrung*. That these are also Eugenie's paramount capacities is clear in "Pfand der Libe" in lines 6-7 and in the erotic significance of the rose to which she is paralleled throughout the octave and with which she is identified in line 1. Death will destroy her, as he destroyed the advocate in sonnet I/XX, at the very center of her being.

Neither the preservation of Eugenie's personal integrity—and thus of her human dignity—in line 8 nor the essential destruction represented here implies an explicitly personal defeat. What emerges in the strophe is less the destruction of Eugenie than destruction itself. Eugenie is involved in the process only in her capacity as an example. None of her personal characteristics, no personal effort on her part is ever mentioned. All that we learn of her person is that she is loved and honored. These attributes do not distinguish her unique person. Inasmuch as they belong to the tradition of courtly love, they establish the girl as a representative of an idealized female type. Since she is destroyed precisely in these representative capacities, the defeat accomplished in line 8 is not uniquely personal; it is typical. Both the destruction described in the second quatrain and the particular defeat entailed by this destruction are representative.

The sestet is little changed, but the profound revision of the octave alters the function of the last strophes. In the Lissa version the thrust of the argument is not entirely clear. The most important point made in the octave is that the girl's beauty will be corrupted, and this alone would seem to motivate the sigh from which the poet takes his departure. The reference to beauty in line 10 associates itself with the girl, for this quality has been ascribed to her explicitly. Line 12 would appear then to transfer the quality from the girl to the flower. It is by no means evident that the poet is not dwelling still on the girl's susceptibility to death and decay, and that the point made in line 11 and developed in the second tercet does not continue to argue her corruptibility. If the poet has moved here to a larger aspect of his argument, the prosecution is clumsy. Lines 9-10 bring the first indication that temporality is a general phenomenon. In this proximity to a major enlargement of the focus, an important extension of the argument in line 11—from the visible world at large to mankind in particular and from simple mortality to pervasive death—appears as an afterthought. "Die Blum" in line 12 is ambiguous. The definite article may be either generic or specific. Whether this is a reference to the rose in line 2 is not clear. If it is, a new quality is introduced to the flower. The symbol as it was established in the first strophe is not competent for the function required of it here. In line 14 an imperfect parallel fails to draw the intended analogy between the rose and mankind. In default of the analogy, the line simply repeats the extension of the argument in line 11.

In the final version the outlines of the argument are perfectly plain. Having finished with the illustrative example in the second quatrain, the poet adverts to the larger point stated in line 4. He returns to the mainstream of his demonstration, enters his plea once more, and reinforces his point by recapitulating. Line 10, with its references to beauty, permanence, and color, suggests the example of the rose and applies it now to the visible world at large. In the reference to beauty the connection is particularly secure, for in this version the quality is readily associated with the rose, a paragon among roses (line 3). "Bestand" associates itself somewhat less unambiguously with the flower, but the fact that the rose is said to have disappeared (line 3) helps to establish the link. The relevance of color rests upon common convention. Following the recapitulation, the extension of the argument in line 11 gains prominence and with this prominence, a poignancy proper to the sense of the statement. In line 12 the suggestion of the rose in line 10 is worked out explicitly. The symbol is reintroduced, and in line 13 a representative competence suggested in line 3 ("so unversehns verschwand") is developed to cover the new point made in line 11. Line 14 accomplishes the last step in these successive deductions from one symbolic event. The perfect parallel applies the rose in its full competence to mankind's life in the shadow of death.

Gryphius' integrated sonnets range from the trivial wedding poems to such a statuesque production as the sonnet to Eugenie. In this motleyness a curious discrepancy between the distribution of quality in his work and in Greiffenberg's collection—a discrepancy which appeared already in their respective linear and repetitive sonnets—is confirmed. In Greiffenberg's sonnets there is a direct correlation between her method of composition and the quality of her poems. On the whole, her linear pieces are inferior to her repetitive poems; her amassed poems are inferior to both of these; and her integrated sonnets are superior to all others. Gryphius, on the other hand, produces a full scale of quality in three of these four groups. His linear, repetitive, and integrated sonnets all range from slight pieces to eminently successful compositions. The explanation is that Greiffenberg's collection is a record of her coping with one principal failing—meagerness. She experiments with a number of methods, and in the arrangement of her sonnets here each brings her closer to free and sovereign composition. Gryphius, by contrast, is not embattled with his shortcomings. He is exercising his powers—with mixed success. In each group of poems there are instances of his having worked carelessly. In each group except the unassimilated sonnets there are poems in which he displays his talents to full advantage.

His talents are diverse and considerable. He is blessed first of all with a bounty of appropriate material. He has a highly developed sense for the internal logic of his material. He is discerning about its intellectual potential and quick to identify and to develop its inherent idea. He is astonishingly resourceful in exploiting its connotative capacities. He has a sophisticated ear: he is responsive to rhythms of speech, to gradations of expression, and to rhetorical effects. He is alive to the possibilities of form and astute at using these possibilities to reinforce his idea. He is a master at the arrangement and cogent presentation of an argument. One final talent has enabled Gryphius to take full advantage of all these gifts: he was critical of his own work; he saw its weaknesses and revised.

Greiffenberg was born under a less favorable star. Her difficulty with insufficiency is a grave failing of far-reaching consequences. She must first enlarge the bulk of her material. Only when this step has been accomplished can she think of purification and simplification. Usually she does not reach this second step. She is less than adept at developing the salient points in her material, the ideas with the greatest potential for intellectual or rhetorical development. She has, quite simply, no great aptitude for reduction and clarification, and given her particular creative process, she needs such an aptitude more urgently than Gryphius. Furthermore, her sense of formal grace, whether in the dimensions of the entire sonnet, of the strophe, or of the line alone, is often blunt. For all her extravagant rhyming, the fineness of her ear is not above reproach. Finally, Greiffenberg neglected to revise. Her peculiar means of composition would have made review and refinement of her work particularly desirable.

CHAPTER EIGHT

INSTEAD OF A CONCLUSION

The lyric poetry of the German Baroque has suffered its fair share from the reduction and simplification which attends any attempt to order and interpret the past. Explicit or assumed contrast with the poetry which began to appear late in the eighteenth century has exaggerated the characteristics of the poetry of both periods. Perhaps it is not altogether gratuitous then to call attention to something obvious: Baroque lyric poetry is no more pure convention and tradition than is *Erlebnislyrik* pure inspiration and experience. Both are a combination of conventional practices and unique impulse. In the earlier poetry, as in the later, tradition and impulse are brought together in an act of craftsmanship, of art in the original sense of the word. I am not sure how well served we are any more by the contrast which would have it that the later poetry is original, unique, and inspired, while the earlier is conventional, representative, and fabricated. Poetry in both periods is in some degree original and conventional, unique and representative, inspired and fabricated. I do not mean to belittle the difference between poetry in the two periods. The difference is undeniable and it is important—so important that we need something more finely calibrated than contrast to assess it. I would suggest that it can be represented more adequately as a problem of selection, proportion, and combination among components of poetry common to both periods.

It would follow that Baroque poetry can be represented more fully if we treat it no longer principally with concepts and terms which belong to the theory of *Erlebnislyrik*. I am not sure that a coinage such as "nicht-lyrische Lyrik" is an enduring aid to understanding (Conrady, p. 54). We seem to have reached a point where positing what is called *Erlebnislyrik* as the norm of lyric poetry and the context in which all lyric poetry is to be described encumbers our thought processes more than it expedites them.[1] In any case, definition *ex negativo* and description by contrastive analysis are but perspectives upon this poetry, and these perspectives are more amply represented than other possible per-

---

[1] The awkwardness of this procedure is the subject of a dissertation which deserves more notice than it has received: Ernst Voege, *Mittelbarkeit und Unmittelbarkeit in der Lyrik: Untersuchungen an lyrischen Gedichten des Altertums und der Neuzeit im Hinblick auf die herrschende deutsche Lyrik-Theorie* (München, 1932; republished Darmstadt: Wissenschaftliche Buchgesellschaft, 1968).

spectives. Treating this poetry exclusively as a composite of traditions is also no longer adequate. Again it is less a question of the absolute validity of a certain procedure than of needs in our present state of knowledge. We are not uninformed about the presence of inherited goods, though our knowledge is not complete and must continue to grow. On the other hand, we know virtually nothing about the transformations which took place in the heritage as poets converted it into what we call Baroque poems, and we know virtually nothing about the poetic processes of conversion. Findings on these questions, no less than knowledge of the inherited goods themselves, enlarge our understanding of the period, of its assumptions and outlook, of the terms on which it conceived of itself and responded to human problems. Finally, I am not sure that it is productive any more to handle these texts as if they were mosaics, to lift from them certain constituents—e.g. rhetorical figures, emblematic references, metaphors—for separate treatment. The procedure can take little account of proportion in poetry; it promotes no sense for possible wholeness in this verse. I am less convinced than Conrady (pp. 259-61) that this is poetry in which *Gehalt* and *Gestalt* are predisposed to go their separate ways. The difficulty, I suspect, lies less with the poetry than with our way of looking at it. We have not looked long and patiently enough, or at the right things, to have discovered the terms on which the two meet.

What we need is probably not so much a new method—no method is ever really adequate to literature—as a new attitude. We need more spacious vision, vision which combines an informed sense for the strangeness and remoteness of this period with an organ for its logic and therefore for the potential wholeness of its literature. Here students of the seventeenth century in France and England have exceeded us. Quite likely, the literature of the seventeenth century in France and England also exceeds the German. But is this alone the reason the German Baroque should still be considered bizarre, even among scholars, whereas the French, English, and Americans can feel at home among their poets?

If it is permissible to understand the difference between the poetry of the Baroque and the poetry which appeared late in the eighteenth century as a problem of proportion, what account can one give of the relationship between poetry and poetics in the seventeenth century? Our understanding of both the poetry and the poetics is such that for the time being we should not even hazard a guess. At least we know that the relationship is not as simple as once it was thought to be. As the work of Joachim Dyck, Ludwig Fischer, and Wilfried Barner shows, poetics, no less than poetry, requires interpretation, and we have only just begun.[2]

[2] Joachim Dyck, *Tichtkunst: Deutsche Barockpoetik und rhetorische Tradition* (Bad Homburg, 1966); Ludwig Fischer, *Gebundene Rede: Dichtung und Rhetorik in der literarischen Theorie des Barock in Deutschland* (Tübingen, 1968); Wilfried Barner, *Barockrhetorik: Untersuchungen zu ihren geschichtlichen Grundlagen* (Tübingen, 1970).

Our imperfect understanding of the poetics is one problem; an inevitable discrepancy between poetics and poetry, between the prescription for poetry and the performance of the poets, is another. The solution may not lie only in the poets' putative inability to fulfill the prescriptions. As Barner indicates, it may lie also in the larger context of rhetoric and the purposes rhetoric served. Our rudimentary understanding of all these things is proof enough that we cannot presume to deduce the poetry from the poetics and then to elevate the poetics—as we construe them—as the measure with which we assay the poetry.

The problem of contemporary standards and the problem of the poet's performance bring us to the hardest question of all: at what point does this poetry reach an equilibrium between the claims of its historical provenance and the claims of our contemporary realization of it? Perhaps it comes to rest at no designable point. Part of its fascination is its movement between these realms, so that we apprehend it at once as an exotic and as a movingly familiar address to the human condition. By recognizing these contrary claims and negotiating between them, by exploring the position of poetry between them, I believe we can arrive at a more commensurate understanding and enjoyment of this literature than was possible either when we denied its historical distinctiveness or when we denied our contemporary experience. But it is an intricate maneuver and constantly in need of correction.

BIBLIOGRAPHY

I. PRIMARY SOURCES

Birken, Sigmund von. Papers in the Archiv des Pegnesischen Blumenordens, Germanisches Nationalmuseum, Nürnberg: letters from Catharina and Hans Rudolf von Greiffenberg, Johann Wilhelm von Stubenberg, and others to Birken; drafts of letters from Birken to Catharina and to Caspar von Lilien. 1659-1681. Bundles 6 and 12.

Greiffenberg, Catharina Regina von. *Geistliche Sonnette / Lieder und Gedichte / zu Gottseeligem Zeitvertreib.* Nürnberg, 1662. In the von Faber du Faur Collection of the Beinecke Library, Yale University. (Reprinted with certain emendations under the auspices of the Wissenschaftliche Buchgesellschaft. Darmstadt, 1967.)

―――――――. *Gedichte: Ausgewählt und mit einem Nachwort versehen von Hubert Gersch.* Berlin, 1964.

Gryphius, Andreas. *Freuden / und / Trauer-Spiele / auch / Oden / und / Sonnette.* Breslau, 1663. In the von Faber du Faur Collection of the Beinecke Library, Yale University. (The sonnets, Books I and II, are reprinted in *Andreas Gryphius: Dichtungen,* ed. Karl Otto Conrady, Rowohlts Klassiker, 19. Hamburg, 1968.)

―――――――. *Gesamtausgabe der deutschsprachigen Werke,* ed. Marian Szyrocki and Hugh Powell. Vol. I: *Sonette.* Tübingen, 1963.

II. SECONDARY SOURCES ON GREIFFENBERG

Bircher, Martin and Peter M. Daly. "Catharina Regina von Greiffenberg und Johann Wilhelm von Stubenberg: Zur Frage der Autorschaft zweier anonymer Widmungsgedichte," *Literaturwissenschaftliches Jahrbuch der Görres Gesellschaft,* 7 (1966), 17-35.

Bircher, Martin. *Johann Wilhelm von Stubenberg (1619-1663) und sein Freundeskreis: Studien zur österreichischen Barockliteratur protestantischer Edelleute.* Berlin, 1968.

Black, Ingrid and Peter Maurice Daly. *Gelegenheit und Geständnis: Unveröffentlichte Gelegenheitsgedichte als verschleierter Spiegel des Lebens und Wirkens der Catharina Regina von Greiffenberg.* Bern, 1971.

Daly, Peter Maurice. "Die Metaphorik in den 'Sonetten' der Catharina Regina von Greiffenberg." Diss. Zürich, 1964. .

―――――――. "Emblematic Poetry of Occasional Meditation," *German Life and Letters,* 25 (1972), 126-39.

―――――――. "Emblematische Strukturen in der Dichtung der Catharina Regina von Greiffenberg," *Europäische Tradition und deutscher Literaturbarock: Internationale Beiträge zum Problem von Überleiferung und Umgestaltung,* ed. Gerhart Hoffmeister, pp. 189-222. Bern, 1973.

―――――――. "Vom privaten Gelegenheitsgedicht zur öffentlichen Andachtsbetrachtung (zu C. R. von Greiffenbergs 'Trauer Liedlein')," *Euphorion,* 66 (1972), 308-14.

Fässler, Vereni. *Hell-Dunkel in der barocken Dichtung. Studien zum Hell-Dunkel bei Johann Klaj, Andreas Gryphius und Catharina Regina von Greiffenberg.* Bern, 1971.

Frank, Horst-Joachim. *Catharina Regina von Greiffenberg: Leben und Welt der barocken Dichterin.* Göttingen, 1967.

——————. "Catharina Regina von Greiffenberg: Untersuchungen zu ihrer Persönlichkeit und Sonettdichtung." Diss. Hamburg, 1958.

Herzog, Urs. "Literatur in Isolation und Einsamkeit: Catharina Regina von Greiffenberg und ihr literarischer Freundeskreis," *Deutsche Vierteljahrsschrift für Literaturwissenschaft und Geistesgeschichte,* 45 (1971), 515-46.

Schürk, Ingrid. "'Sey dennoch unverzagt': Zwei barocke Sonette von der Bewältigung des Schicksals," *Aus der Welt des Barock,* ed. Richard Alewyn et al. Stuttgart, 1957.

Slocum, Malve Kristin. "Untersuchungen zu Lob und Spiel in den Sonetten der Catharina Regina von Greiffenberg." Diss. Cornell, 1971.

Sullivan, John H. "The German Religious Sonnet of the Seventeenth Century." Diss. Berkeley, 1966.

Uhde-Bernays, Hermann. "Catharina Regina von Greiffenberg: Ein Beitrag zur Geschichte des deutschen Lebens und Dichtens im 17. Jahrhundert." Diss. Berlin, 1903.

Villiger, Leo. "Catharina Regina von Greiffenberg: Zu Sprache und Welt der barocken Dichterin." Diss. Zürich, 1952.

Wehrli, Max. "Catharina Regina von Greiffenberg," *Schweizerische Monatshefte,* 45 (September 1965), 577-82.

Wiedemann, Conrad. "Engel, Geist und Feuer: Zum Dichterselbstverständnis bei Klaj, Greiffenberg und Kuhlmann, *Literatur und Geistesgeschichte: Festgabe für Heinz Otto Burger,* ed. Reinhold Grimm and Conrad Wiedemann, pp. 85-109. Berlin, 1968.

III. OTHER SECONDARY SOURCES

Arendt, Dieter. "Andreas Gryphius' Eugenien-Gedichte," *Zeitschrift für deutsche Philologie,* 87 (May 1968), 161-79.

Barner, Wilfried. *Barockrhetorik: Untersuchungen zu ihren geschichtlichen Grundlagen.* Tübingen, 1970.

Benjamin, Walter. *Ursprung des deutschen Trauerspiels.* Rev. ed. Frankfurt, 1963.

Beckmann, Adelheid. *Motive und Formen der deutschen Lyrik des 17. Jahrhunderts.* Tübingen, 1960.

Booth, Stephen. *An Essay on Shakespeare's Sonnets.* New Haven, 1969.

Brooke-Rose, Christine. *A Grammar of Metaphor.* 2nd ed. London, 1965.

Cohen, Fritz. "Two Early Sonnets of Andreas Gryphius: A Study of their Original and Revised Forms," *German Life and Letters,* 25 (1972), 115-26.

Conrady, Karl Otto. *Lateinische Dichtungstradition und deutsche Lyrik des 17. Jahrhunderts.* Bonn, 1962.

Curtius, Ernst Robert. *Europäische Literatur und lateinisches Mittelalter.* Bern, 1948.

Dyck, Joachim. *Tichtkunst: Deutsche Barockpoetik und rhetorische Tradition.* Bad Homburg, 1966.

Fechner, Jörg-Ulrich, ed. *Das deutsche Sonett.* München, 1969.
Fischer, Ludwig. *Gebundene Rede: Dichtung und Rhetorik in der literarischen Theorie des Barock in Deutschland.* Tübingen, 1968.
Fricke, Gerhard. *Die Bildlichkeit in der Dichtung des Andreas Gryphius.* Berlin, 1933.
Gaster, Theodor H., ed. *The New Golden Bough: A New Abridgement of Sir James Frazer's Classic Work.* New York, 1959.
Henkel, Arthur and Albrecht Schöne. *Emblemata: Handbuch zur Sinnbildkunst des XVI. und XVII. Jahrhunderts.* Stuttgart, 1967.
Jöns, Dietrich Walter. *Das "Sinnen-Bild": Studien zur allegorischen Bildlichkeit bei Andreas Gryphius.* Stuttgart, 1966.
Koch, Franz. *Goethe und Plotin.* Leipzig, 1925.
Martz, Louis. *The Poetry of Meditation.* New Haven, 1954.
Manheimer, Victor. *Die Lyrik des Andreas Gryphius.* Berlin, 1904.
Mönch, Walter. *Das Sonett: Gestalt und Geschichte.* Heidelberg, 1955.
Pyritz, Hans. *Paul Flemings Liebeslyrik: Zur Geschichte des Petrarkismus.* Göttingen, 1963.
Schindler, Marvin S. *Sonnets of Andreas Gryphius: Use of the Poetic Word in the Seventeenth Century.* Gainesville, 1971.
Schöne, Albrecht. *Emblematik und Drama im Zeitalter des Barock.* München, 1964.
Spahr, Blake Lee. *The Archives of the Pegnesischer Blumenorden: A Survey and Reference Guide.* Berkeley, 1960.
Strich, Fritz. "Der lyrische Stil im 17. Jahrhundert," *Abhandlungen zur deutschen Literaturgeschichte. Franz Muncker zum 60. Geburtstag dargebracht.* München, 1916. Reprinted in *Deutsche Barockforschung,* ed. Richard Alewyn, pp. 229-59. Köln, 1965.
Trunz, Erich. "Fünf Sonette des Andreas Gryphius: Versuch einer Auslegung," *Vom Geist der Dichtung: Gedächtnisschrift für Robert Petsch,* ed. Fritz Martini, pp. 180-205. Hamburg, 1949.
Warnke, Frank J. *European Metaphysical Poetry.* New Haven, 1961.
——————. *Versions of Baroque.* New Haven, 1972.
Wellek, René and Austin Warren. *Theory of Literature.* Rev. ed. New York, 1965.
Welti, Heinrich. *Geschichte des Sonettes in der deutschen Dichtung.* Leipzig, 1884.
Weydt, Günther. "Sonettkunst des Barock: Zum Problem der Umarbeitung bei Andreas Gryphius," *Jahrbuch der deutschen Schiller Gesellschaft,* 9 (1965), 1-32.
Windfuhr, Manfred. *Die barocke Bildlichkeit und ihre Kritiker.* Stuttgart, 1966.

INDEX OF SONNETS
GREIFFENBERG AND GRYPHIUS

A. CATHARINA VON GREIFFENBERG

6	Eiferige Lobes vermahnung 15n., 42n.
9	Demütiger Entschluß / GOtt zu loben 15n., 90-93, 95
10	Von der hohen Erschaffungs Gnade 42
16	Auf GOttes Herrliche Wunder Regirung 38n.
17	GOTTes Vorsehungs-Spiegel 24-27, 32
19	Gedanken des Großglaubigen Abrahams 37n.
20	Deßen Danksgedanken / bey unverhoffter Entsetzung 37n.
23	Freud schallender Ausspruch / des wunderlich geführten Josephs 36-39
25	Auf die süßeste Gnaden-Erquickung 42n.
27	Der GOttes-Wunder Erklingung / von dem GOtt geleiteten Mose 35-36, 37
28	Auf meinen Vorsatz / die Heilige Schrifft zulesen 94n.
30	Uber des Glaubens Krafft: Bey der Israelitischen Meer-Wunder Reise 94n.
31	Uber die Allmacht-erscheinende Meer-Reise der Israeliter 45n.
32	Uber die GOttes-Gnadentrieffende Wüsten 45n.
34	Auf die GOtt-beliebende Glaubens stärke 15n., 90, 93-95
35	Auf eben dieselbe / und Göttlichen wortes Krafft 86
36	Die verharrende Hoffnung 15n.
37	Auf meine / auf Gottes Gnad gerichtete / unabläßliche Hoffnung 59-61
43	Das beglückende Unglück 40-43, 48
47	Uber GOttes unbegreiffliche Regirung / seiner Kirchen und Glaubigen 11n., 15n.
48	Auf eben dieselbige 94n.
49	Uber mein Symb. oder gedenkspruch. W. G. W. 27
54	Auf die Thränen 44, 46, 48
55	Auf eben dieselben 44-46, 47, 48, 49
56	Auch über die Thränen 44
57	Auf eben selbe 44
60	[Auf das verwirrte widerwärtige aussehen] 20-23, 42n.
61	Uber Gottes regirende Wunderweise 18-20, 22, 23
65	Auf Gottes seltsame Geist-Regirung 99
66	Auf eben selbige 37n.
67	Auf die Göttliche Gnaden- und Wunderhülff-Hoffnung 15n.
68	Auf die unbegreiffliche Glaubens Art 94n.

69	Ruhe der unergründlichen verlangen 50-52	
70	Uber mein unablässliches verlangen und hoffen 15n.	
75	Uber Gottes Wunderführung 17-18, 19, 20, 23, 26, 27, 30	
76	Uber ein zu ruck gegangenes / doch Christlich- und heiliges Vornemen 16, 61-64	
77	Auf berührtes verhindertes Vornehmen 16, 73	
78	Gänzliche Ergeb- und Begebung / in und nach Gottes Willen / in dieser und allen Sachen 16, 78-80	
79	Auf berührte Verhinderniß 16, 62	
80	Auf eben selbe 16, 62	
81	Auch auf selbe Begebnus 16	
82	Uber des Creutzes Nutzbarkeit 45n.	
83	Auf die verfolgte doch ununterdruckliche Tugend 30-32, 39, 40-42	
92	Auf Glückliche Erquick- und Erfreuung 46-49	
93	Auf das Lust-vermehrende Unglück / nach erlangter Errettung 46, 48, 49	
96	Uber ein unverhofft beschertes Hülff-Glück 69-71	
98	Herzlich-vergwistes Vertrauen auf GOtt / in noch nicht völliger Glückes-Besitzung 45	
106	Auf die / der Gottheits-Sonne / aufgehende Freuden-Nacht 56-58	
108	Auf Christus Wunder-Geburt 28-30, 32	
110	[Auf [Christi] Mensch-werdige Wunder-That] 81-83	
113	Auf eben diese Herz-entzuckende Freuden-Geschicht 67	
120	Andere Neu Jahrs Gedanken 73-75, 84	
122	Uber des Allwachenden Schlaf / in dem Wind-bestürmten Schifflein 83-84	
125	An die Cananeische Glaubens-Heldin 45n.	
129	Auf unsers Heilandes Allmacht-durchstrahlten Wunder-Wandel auf dieser Erden 84-87	
130	An die allübertreffende / von keinem Lob nie erreichete Gottes Güte 86	
134	Auf des Traurenden Christi / herz- und schmerzliches Gebet 52-54	
135	Uber den GOtt-schmerzlichen / uns tröstlichen / Leidens- und Erlösungs-Anfang im Oelgarten 48	
148	Uber das Wort: Er ward ein Fluch am Holz 32-35, 39	
150	Auf sein allerheiligstes Blutvergiessen 49	
164	Das dritte [in dem Tod Christi geschehene / Zeichen]: Das Erd-beben 64-66, 68	
165	Das vierdte: Die Felsen Zerreissung 45n.	
170	[Auf die Frölich- und Herrliche Auferstehung Christi] 76-78, 87, 89	

171	Auf die / den Weibern offenbarte / Auferstehung 73	
186	An den wehrtesten Herzens-Schatz / den Heiligen Geist 45n.	
188	Auf des Heiligen Geistes Wunder-Trost 48, 91n.	
195	Uber die Allerheiligste Göttliche Dreyeinigkeit 66-68	
196	Auf eben dieselbige 67	
201	H. Neuer Jahrs-Wunsch 15n.	
205	Einfältig / doch Allvermögende Glaubenskrafft 94n.	
209	Als durch eines H. Mannes Leibeigenschafft / die Landschafft / in welche er verkaufft / vermittelst seiner Predigt bekehret wurde 94n.	
210	Als mir einmal / am H. Drey König Abend / beym Eyrgiessen / der HErr Christus am Creutz klar und natürlich erschienen / oder aufgefahren 15n., 81, 83	
217	Dämpfung der unzeitigen Tugend-Regung 21n.	
222	Auf den / GOtt Lob! vergehenden Winter 49	
223	GOtt-lobende Frülings-Lust 88-89	
225	GOtt-lobende Frülings-Lust 84, 87-90	
229	GOtt-lobende Frülings-Lust 84	
245	Gänzliche Ergebung in GOttes Willen 15n.	
246	Auf die unaufhörliche GOttes- und Tugend-Liebe 15n.	
250	Uber die Unendlichkeit Gottes 42	

B. ANDREAS GRYPHIUS
(I/III designates Book I, Sonnet III)

	[An eine hohen Standes Jungfraw] 113-118	
I/III	Uber die Geburt JEsu 56-58	
I/IV	Uber des HErrn Gefängnüß 97	
I/IX	Thränen in schwerer Kranckheit 105	
I/XI	Menschliches Elende 7, 98, 108-11, 112	
I/XII	Tumulus admodum Reverend. Excellentis. Viri PAULI GRYPHII, THEOLOGI 98	
I/XIV	In Bibliothecam Nobiliß. Ampliß̃imique Viri GEORGII SCHONBORNERI 98	
I/XV	PAULI GRYPHII, PHILOSOPHI & Theologi Fratris dulciss. Exilium 98-102	
I/XX	Grabschrifft eines trefflichen Vorsprechers 106-08, 112	
I/XXII	An Eugenien 113, 114-18	
I/XXIII	Auff Herrn Joachimi Spechts Medici, Hochzeit 112, 113	
I/XXV	Auff H. Godofredi Eichorns und Rosine Stoltzin Hochzeit 112	
I/XLIV	Grab-Schrifft / der Jungfrauschafft 97	
I/XLV	Thränen in schwerer Kranckheit 105	
I/XLVIII	An sich selbst 105-06, 108	

I/XLIX	An die Welt 97
I/L	Uber seines Herrn Bruder P. GRYPHII Grab 98, 100-03, 105
II/VII	SIcut uri nata ligna . . . 97
II/IX	Johannis Chrysostomi Worte 97
II/X	Uberschrifft an dem Tempel der Sterbligkeit 98
II/XXI	Auff H. Ditterich Baums und Jungfr. Annae Mariae Gryphiae Hochzeit 112
II/XXIX	Auff H. Sigmund Gutsche / Raths-Verwandten zu Freystadt 112
II/XXX	H. Eliae AEbelii und Jungfr. Barbarae Gerlachin Hochzeit 112
II/XXXI	H. Nathanael Roßteuscher und Alithaeae Roussiae Hochzeit 112
II/XXXII	Auff Herrn Herings Hochzeit 112
II/XXXIX	Auff einen ungeschickten Römer 98
II/XL	An CLEANDRUM 97
II/XLI	Als Er aus Rom geschidn 98
II/XLVI	Der Tod 112
II/XLVII	Das Letzte Gerichte 103-05

www.ingramcontent.com/pod-product-compliance
Lightning Source LLC
Chambersburg PA
CBHW031316150426
43191CB00005B/254